D1603752

# SOM
# journal

# 8

HATJE
CANTZ

# Contents

# On Teamwork: Standards and Practices
## Peter MacKeith

In November 2011, the professional jury appointed to review SOM projects for recognition in *SOM Journal* 8 met for three days in the Abbaye Royaumont, a thirteenth-century French monastery some twenty-five miles north of Paris. The Abbaye had been converted from its religious purposes already at the time of the French Revolution, and since the nineteen-fifties has been a conference center for business, governmental, and cultural events.

The SOM 8 jury—architect Einar Jarmund of the well-recognized Oslo-based practice Jarmund-Vigsnæs, urban designer Oliver Schulze, design director of Gehl Architects—Urban Quality Consultants of Copenhagen, and Rob Diemer, director at In Posse, a leading environmental consulting practice, based in Philadelphia—convened in the Abbaye and reviewed twenty-eight SOM projects in the intense quietude of the former monastery. The setting for the jury inspired concentration and dialogue, reflection and common outlooks: the deliberative process was productively congenial and collaborative. The jury ultimately selected six among the range of submitted projects for particular recognition this year in the pages of this journal. The nature of the jury's observations and evaluations are described in the second half of this introduction, but the jury's location was more notably intentional for the purposes of the contents of *SOM Journal* 8 and bears further elaboration.

While previous jury deliberations have usually been held outside of the SOM offices in order to declare a clear independence of the review process, most of the juries have been organized to occur in (or near) a significant work of modern architecture, in locations intended to provide physical inspiration: Charles Rennie Mackintosh's Glasgow School of Art or Alvar Aalto's Maison Carré, for instance. The Abbaye Royaumont has no such obvious pedigree or effect, however, and yet its choice was neither historicist, whimsical, nor fortuitous. The Abbaye was, in fact, the location of a significant event in the history of modern architecture and urban design, namely the first declarative meeting of the CIAM breakaway group of modern architects, urban designers, and design thinkers who, despite their internal differences, came to be known collectively as Team 10.

As *SOM Journal* 8 contributor, and urban design historian, Eric Mumford points out in his thorough essay detailing that first meeting, Team 10 may have never been properly a "team," more of a loose affiliation of younger architects and urban designers unhappy with the directions and directives of a Gropius and Le Corbusier-led CIAM. However, the power and suggestiveness of its purported team-based approach—advocating more intimate, more dynamic, more "humane" planning processes and solutions to address postwar conditions of urban development and renewal, housing, and infrastructure—remain a strong presence in our inheritance of modern architecture. The ambition in our jury's return to the Abbaye Royaumont—the scene of a dramatic Team 10 meeting seeking new modes of design leadership—was to reinforce to the jury, to those who had submitted work for review, and to our readers, the thematic emphases of this number of the *SOM Journal* and the one following: teamwork, collaboration, and design leadership.

Architecture, undeniably of course, has ever been—to use the prevalent contemporary qualifiers—a collaborative, interdisciplinary, team-based endeavor. The complexity of the architect and urban designer's tasks and responsibilities render the importance of these qualities and approaches self-evident. Yet, the more persistent, popular, and dominant models and reputations remain those of the architect-as-artist, or the architect-as-sole practitioner, or the "hero-architect," a charismatic figure providing singular, distinctive, individual expressions of architectural brilliance and cultural identity. The professional and public challenges posed by conceptions of teamwork, collaboration, and design leadership are

Clockwise from top left: Einar Jarmund, Peter MacKeith, Robert Diemer, and Oliver Schulze outside the Abbaye Royaumont, November 19, 2011

important to examine as historical developments, to be sure, but also as elements of contemporary professional practice.

The near past of the post-World War II period, so affected by the immensity of the architecture and urban design tasks to be addressed, saw the clear emergence of important collaborative understandings and corporate organizational models into modern architectural practice—in educational approaches, in professional practice structures and nomenclatures, in the professional and cultural institutions (museums, congresses, and unions of architects, professional and academic journals). Equally, work with and on behalf of governments, corporations, and industries led architects to productive engagements with larger organizational models and with team-based research-and-development approaches to architectural solutions and structural and material innovations.

In her *SOM Journal* 8 essay, architectural historian Eeva-Liisa Pelkonen highlights the emergences of these modes of architectural practices in the postwar period; citing an emblematic case study, she describes the structure and approach of first Eero Saarinen and Associates, and then the post-Saarinen practice of Kevin Roche John Dinkeloo Architects, as both offices developed new materials for their architecture in conjunction with a variety of industries and manufacturers. Here, Eero Saarinen and Associates and SOM have complementary roles on the postwar architectural stage of form and space and purpose and technology; Professor Pelkonen's study of a practice seemingly centered on the bravura of its titular principal—both ESA and KRJDA were in fact highly organized corporate practices—provides the implicit useful comparison with SOM's own emergence in the same time period and its own focus on innovative research and development, on productive governmental, corporate, and industrial partnerships, and on distinctive design at all scales.

SOM and Saarinen's research and achievements in architectural technologies—in new materials, innovative structures, and movement systems, for instance—emphasized collaborative practice, to be sure, but also privileged technological advancement with a tangible, durable character. In a fascinating study, however, Nicholas Adams undertakes the exploration of SOM research into less visible technologies, although ones by no means less prescient in their ambitions. His essay follows SOM's initiation of research and development into digital technologies (both hardware and software), and the firm's subsequent deployment of those technologies into design engineering, building analysis, and visual documentation applications, bridges from the postwar period to the verge of the present day. Adams's study, based on extensive employee interviews and archival research, continues his attentive narrative of SOM's history, which he has written about over several issues of the *Journal*. In harmony with the emphases of this number though, his essay provides more than a chronology of events: the narrative of SOM's efforts to develop and define digital technologies is a narrative of friendships and shared ideals, of collaborative research and team-based labor. That the effort ultimately did not lead to full deployment and success speaks less of the process within SOM and more of the collaborative efforts of others elsewhere in the hardware and software industries. In Adams's essay, the human factor of the SOM effort is palpable—and laudable.

In the present day, in which the public (at least) perceives architecture as a bipolar profession, constituted in large part as an anonymous service industry, but given effervescent, near-manic distinction by an over-arching constellation of "star-architects," each practicing in distinctive "signature" styles, the conceptions of teamwork, collaboration and collective design leadership can slip away all too easily under pressures of ego, marketing tools and public relations—or so it might seem. *Metropolis* magazine editor Susan Szenasy describes the current moment in her essay as "the age of collaboration," and finds this quality ubiquitous and essential, even in contemporary practices otherwise understood as Saarinen's was—as a signature practice. Her experience following the design and construction of Rem Koolhaas/OMA's Seattle Public Library was instructive in this regard, and subverted many commonly held perceptions of the Koolhaas design process and consequent building resolution. In a performance-centered, evidence-based design age, as constrained by economic as much as environmental considerations, heroic gestures and signature styles mean little without the collaborative team-based substance of research, consultation, and construction.

This understanding is underscored suggestively in the *Journal*'s final essay, "Teamwork in Practice," in fact, a discussion between principal designers Michael Bierut of Pentagram and Sandy Speicher of IDEO, focusing on their respective firms' collaborative approaches and interdisciplinary design practices. The essay is itself an exercise in collaboration across the design culture, with the ambition to draw upon the wisdom of those engaged in modes of design practice different from that of SOM, either in scale of architectural practice, or in design character all together. The essay is based on the belief that architecture can always learn more for its own sustenance from other creative fields, whether they be visual, literary, or design oriented. Directed discussions with Michael Bierut and Sandy Speicher produced engaging perceptions of the challenges and value of collaborative work, ranging from the perceptions of "signature-less" practice to the development of firm-wide cultures of teamwork. Bierut's observes a productive "tension between independence and collectivism" in Pentagram's office structure and work, and Speicher's asserts the "humility, support of creativity, and a belief in collective wisdom deeply embedded in IDEO's culture"; both practices thrive without "a name on the door" by virtue of these methods and approaches.

These essays can be read against the backdrop of the projects submitted by SOM offices worldwide for juried evaluation and given representation here. As outlined at the outset of this introduction, the jury assembled for *SOM Journal* 8 enjoyed a quietly didactic setting and the discussions among the jury members were spirited, good-humored, and productive for all concerned. In keeping with common practice, the editor and managing editor served only as facilitators for the jury evaluations, either through organization of the jury schedule or through moderation and encouragement of the jury discussions. The jury proceedings were recorded and fully transcribed, but the publication of the full transcription is not provided here, an approach first adopted in *SOM Journal* 5. Rather, the jury commentary has been transcribed and edited into a series of project-specific composite statements to provide more coherent evaluations to the design teams.

As practitioners, the jury members were hesitant to venture into more authoritative critically written statements. However, as a group, the jury sounded a number of consistent observations throughout the evaluation process, a set of perceptions and concerns that were stimulated initially by the review of SOM projects and then at a later stage, through reflections on the current state of architecture, urban design, and environmental engineering. The relation between the SOM projects at hand and the larger context of architectural culture and the world economy was very much in the jury's mind throughout the discussions.

The legacy of SOM's firm history and its contributions to architecture have established strong qualitative expectations: an elegance of architectural form, with a focus on structural innovation, supported by in-depth research and a comprehensive outlook and professional services. The jury's review noted several distinctive examples of the continuing SOM concentration on tall-building design (the subject of *SOM Journal* 7), but also several examples of distinctive design in cultural, educational, and public buildings, less wedded to commercial imperatives. But as successive juries have noted, SOM's increasing engagement with master-planning projects for urban districts, university campuses, and governmental complexes highlights its urban design and landscape architecture approaches. The jury was most attentive to issues of contextual response and human scale in these regards—specifically, the scale, movement, and occupation of people at street level and throughout buildings and settings—and most appreciative of those designs that acknowledged and addressed these issues in an

integrated, persuasive manner. Equally, the jury recognized the vital role of landscape architectural design at this scale, and valued those projects which proposed designs with well-researched ecological depth and sensitivity. Given the world's increasing urbanization and the proliferation of "informal settlements," and given the simultaneous pressure on natural resources, water chief among them, there can only be great value in these practice emphases of urban design and landscape architecture.

Throughout the deliberations, the jury also acknowledged the essential, even determining, role of technology in contemporary practice: the powerful presence of digital technologies, of course, but in parallel with SOM's continuing commitment to structural innovation, the evident new frontier is in the research and development of environmental systems and environmentally responsive design. Here, and throughout the practice, SOM's research-based culture provides clear strength and continued potential.

Writing recently in *The Art-Architecture Complex,* the historian and critic Hal Foster concentrates his primary architectural attentions on the work of Richard Rogers, Norman Foster, and Renzo Piano—all exemplars of what he terms "global styles"—and considers the contemporary three the equivalent of "the International Style" modernist representatives: Gropius, Le Corbusier, and Mies van der Rohe.[1] While Foster (the critic) indicates an awareness of the superficial mask each of his "global" architects provides for what are in fact immense organized webs of architects, engineers, and consultants, he cannot help presenting a succession of works of contemporary architecture as individual expressions and achievements. While this is but one example—and certainly not definitive—in such ways, the fiction of privileged authorship is maintained as much in critical cultural discourse as it is through more public and popular methods and outlets.

There is an alternate history of architecture and design to be presented, documented, examined, and critiqued: the architecture and design that emerges out of teamwork, out of design collaboration, and design leadership, relying on multiple streams of information, knowledge, and wisdom. Such a history, such an appreciation, by definition would be not one of individuals, but more of collaborative enterprises, cultures, and societies. It is both a history and an ongoing contemporary narrative, of course, and one that requires many contributions and many advocates, but it is nonetheless an essential comprehension to bring forward into the profession, into architectural education, and into the public mind. Such is the understated ambition of this number of the *SOM Journal* and of the one following, which will focus more fixedly on the idea of design leadership and authorship.

The conception and production of *SOM Journal* 8 relies on such collaborative enterprise. The initiative, support, counsel, and encouragement of editorial board members Luis Fernández Galliano and Joan Ockman have been essential, as has been the wisdom of outgoing editor Juhani Pallasmaa. The attentive and responsible work of jury members Einar Jarmund, Oliver Schulze, and Rob Diemer provided for a sound, thorough review of the SOM project entries. Contributing essayists Eric Mumford, Eeva-Liisa Pelkonen, Susan Szenasy, Nicholas Adams, and design practice respondents Sandy Speicher and Michael Bierut, must all be recognized for their time, energy, and thought. Amy Gill has been a patient, steadfast managing editor throughout the entire process. Lastly, appreciation and admiration must be given to the architects, designers, consultants, and staff of the SOM offices who participate in this firm-wide collaborative effort, and whose work is represented in small and large ways in these pages.

1   Hal Foster, *The Art-Architecture Complex* (London and Brooklyn: 2011), p. viii.

# Jury Observations

## 1 New Blackfriars
London, United Kingdom

Out of the twenty-eight projects submitted, this project grew the most in appreciated value over the course of the review by the entire jury; one member suggested that the project review was a process of "falling more and more in love." The initial misgivings may have had something to do with the way SOM represents a project's key images: there's always a strong focus on the iconic tower. The real virtues of the project have little to do with the tower and everything to do with what happens closer to the street level.

In many ways, the jury felt that 1 New Blackfriars is a project that could not be made by a European architect or practice, even though London is the largest city in Europe. Though 1 New Blackfriars is a very compact project built into an area that is not known yet for its density, this is a fairly upscale development strategy that really makes sense. In the most positive sense of the description, the project takes an "American" or almost "Chicagoan" quality and adds a very convincing American "punch" into the heart of London and the European city structure.

Therefore, this project needs to be considered less as a tower project than as a master plan with multiple buildings, giving great consideration to the relationship those buildings have to each other. Retail, for example, is considered something that makes a positive contribution to the street network. The complex urban character creates a district that is more than the sum of its building components: the sign of a great master plan. There's not too much focus given to the street scenes in the presentation, but they are commendably believable. New buildings come together with existing buildings, everything is activated on the ground plane, not below, and the entire design creates a nice, dense, urban situation.

As initially presented, the depths and accomplishments of the project are not immediately clear. Only when the design of the ground plane becomes clear—when it is possible to comprehend walking through this area—is the full value of the design appreciable. Circulation has been placed on a diagonal to open up different view corridors, to engage Tate Modern, and also to weave through the existing train tracks. At the street level these patterns create new life; as the choreographed movement extends down to the river it really has the potential to add to the destination in a very positive way, and enliven that entire section of the river Thames.

The tower itself has some resemblance to the massing of the Willis Tower (formerly Sears), but the project overall works on so many different levels, with a related variety of geometries. The design manages to weave the fabric of the city together in a convincing way. This credibility and thoroughness continues in the detailing of the façades, producing a richness that differentiates the uses of buildings' occupants. Anyone who has walked from central London, south across the Thames to Tate Modern will know that there is a big gap in city life at this point currently. This design fits its site and the needs of the district quite nicely; it's a satisfying terminus on the southern edge of Blackfriars Bridge. It's a very strong and nearly diagrammatic interpretation of a concept. Of all the projects, this is the most logical in its positive contribution to the ground plane. It not only suits London, but also contributes to what's happening in the city, one that has made great progress in understanding how to use outdoor spaces.

## Seoul Light DMC Tower
Seoul, South Korea

This project represents an important departure point for SOM, in their ongoing definition of super-tall towers, moving from the realm of structural influence to mechanical services and environmental impact. While the ideas and concepts expressed here may not prove out in reality, the study and inclusion of them in this project is an important step for SOM. This study could define a new way of thinking about towers at SOM, in which the importance of structure is emphasized and expressed, but now to be combined with the environmental aspects of the building. Indeed, we could say that while the structural emphasis addresses the idea of gravity, this will be paralleled also by the desire to give the buildings a smaller environmental impact.

This tower provides powerful examples of this thinking through its utilization of vertical spaces and surfaces for both air movement and power generation, from integrated turbines and integrated photovoltaics, to the use of the air movement and breathing green walls to clean the air. While all are important features, the challenge is to not be overwhelmed by these ideas, to remain rational. Another challenge with this building type is that it is inherently very hard to make a case for sustainability, and this project represents an important departure for SOM in that it can really start to study how to achieve that goal. This examination and attempt at integration is commendable.

If the Poly-International was the classic SOM building it could, in some ways, be achieved by a small group, but this all-light tower seems to be quite a different task. It is one so complex that only a truly collaborative effort could control all of this knowledge in such a complex program. This is an important project as it goes to the core of SOM in finding a way to engage the master themes that our building and planning cultures are thinking about today: how towers relate to questions of sustainability. However, we need to be clear: this tower is a study, and does not pursue the full logic of the first two tower projects in Beijing and London. In both of those situations, the tower design is a logical answer to the site's constraints and its opportunities. The challenge here is to define a sustainable tower, and in this effort one of the lessons of the last decade is that sustainability is not just a question of climatic performance and energy use, but also has a strong social component. This is a critical issue for SOM as it shows the weaknesses of the tower typology.

For instance, in the vertical zoning of this project, just because a super-tall tower has five different uses on top of each other does not mean that those uses are integrated. In the tower typology, an additive system is not necessarily an integrated system. Thus, if the question is how to integrate five different types of land and activity, the true integration may well occur in the kind of human settlement forms surrounding the tower. Again, it's critical for SOM to review this but with a heightened regard for a deeper social sustainability. In certain aspects, the designers have thought about this issue (there is a panel proposing a vertical street), but in a tower, these attempts often create a vertical cul-de-sac. The design of places of exchange where people meet need to result in much more than a "dent" in an atrium where people can have a simple visual connection with each other. The city is about meeting the people you want to meet, but also meeting all sorts of other people that you had no intention of encountering. The super tower typology doesn't guarantee you that richness.

It's important for SOM if they're going to retain their leadership in super-tall building to recognize their mastery of the art of integration of structure and architecture. On this basis, SOM can vigorously research and consider the social aspects of super-tall towers and the environmental and services aspect of super-tall towers. This tower is an attempt to start engaging those issues and trying to resolve them satisfactorily, but is by no means a complete resolution.

The 1 New Blackfriars project demonstrated a different attitude toward context, a different attitude toward street life. The visualizations of the eight floors of retail space at the base of the DMC tower are inward looking, mall-like spaces that withdraw themselves from the surroundings rather than contributing to them. 1 New Blackfriars inverted that approach and starts to deal with the master plan of an area. There is room here for comparison and review between the designers of these two projects.

In the complex program of connecting all of these different programs there is opportunity. On higher floors in this building there are visually connecting meeting points, creating the potential for an architecture in itself. This tower, in terms of its architectural language, is a departure from what we know of SOM in that DMC is more of a willfully designed object. Does its imagery derive from somewhere other than its own structure? In the Poly International Plaza project, the general skill level in making a structurally based architecture is quite high; in the DMC, that same level of competence is not so fully achieved.

The structural excellence expected of SOM is not as readily apparent here, it's not an element of the design. One must wonder if the design is derived from the attempt to modulate the environmental aspects or whether it comes from some other place—we would like to understand it as an attempt to address these issues. This proposal is admirable; SOM's success will be in achieving the same level of competence in execution that they have achieved in the integration of systems and structure.

## King Abdullah Financial District Conference Center
Riyadh, Saudi Arabia

Kuwait and Oman possess some of the great cities of the Arab world, but there are both architectural practice and environmental challenges in this region. It is near tragic that, to a certain extent, the traditional Arab building cultures have lost their innate ability to create structures that can deal with the local climate extremes and to create urban places that actually reflect and accommodate the complex social structures of those societies. These nations often rely on outside intelligence to inform their transportation systems and building projects; more often than not, these countries' urban design efforts are associated with power plays and an aggressive form of city building.

This lasting, admirable ambition of this project is of a place where it's not just about arriving by car and then somehow getting into an air-conditioned space; it actually does try to create this intermediate world through a semi-conditioned "tent," in which climate is not removed or not conditioned to being neutralized, rather it is simply mediated. This is a smart approach mechanically, environmentally, and ultimately socially: recycling air-conditioned air from a cooled building and using it to create a semi-air-conditioned world that is better than the climate that surrounds it. The approach will open up opportunities for people to meet and to have the kind of random urban quality that isn't heavily programmed. This is commendable.

Of course, SOM is known for its expertise in towers and the submitted entries provide ample evidence of this. But SOM are also masters at solving complicated programs

and relationships like conference centers. According to the master plan for this district, there is a requirement to work with segmented facades and segmented envelopes in each building. The SOM team appears to have used advanced computer technology to actually work with a very normative way of designing a building envelope. SOM is quite courageous in investing in this research and in applying it in the context of buildings that will get built.

This is going to be an exciting building. What is notable is that the design culture of SOM with its structurally derived architecture has been pushed towards something else in this project. The mediation of the strong Arabic sun has been accomplished in a much more abstracted way in this project than in others that attempt to flirt with Arabic patterns and so on. In this project, the whole complexity of the envelope is derived from its structure. Looking at these interiors, it is clear that this project is going to be an exciting space to move through. The project uses the enclosure as opposed to the screen to create a modulated space outside of the conditioned envelope. This tactic allows for an environment that is more welcoming than just a screening solution alone. The enclosure is developed as a rather unique form and with a unique pattern using some iterations of solar insulation as well as rotated panels. However, the totality reads as a unique idea as opposed to something familiar, and stands out on these merits. The sketch on the first page of the presentation—of the tent-like enclosure—has that quality, one that appealed to all on the jury.

The sort of technological skill that a practice like SOM can bring to bear on such a project is enviable. This project seems to be a result of a long-term culture of research embedded in SOM.

## The Planning of Four Villages on University Island
Guangzhou, China

It might come as a surprise to some that SOM does a significant amount of work not related to the highrise towers and other building types historically associated with the practice. This larger-scale, urban design and landscape architecture aspect of the firm's work is lesser known, but obviously an important and still-growing element in their portfolio. The practice is quite heavily engaged in planning projects and master-planning and regional planning initiatives worldwide and the jury reviewed a gamut of responses from across the world. A large number of projects are being undertaken in rapidly growing countries such as China, where urbanization is undergoing record development.

Among this larger portfolio of master-planning and urban design, the jury had great appreciation for the project the Four Villages on University Island. A common criticism of international practice is that such a practice's designs possess an evident superficiality, based on an inability to engage and understand a local context. The Four Villages proposal is commendable for its sensitivity to the local context. This project is premised on an honest engagement with the social and physical structure that is found in the pre-existing four villages within the larger site; these underlying contextual structures have been intelligently explored. The investigations discovered that there is a natural system for parks and important landmark buildings, and a compelling landscape narrative of different ponds and paths.

The proposal thus animates with distinction the idea that the experience of cities is not all about large area planning. Instead, the urban and landscape experience is really about understanding how inhabitants move through cities and landscapes to experience them. The Four Villages plan creates such a "pedestrian friendly" environment, but one actually related to existing landscape features. This sensitivity demonstrates that this is more than skin-deep as an exploration of context and those qualities are then lifted into the new plans.

The proposal's renderings demonstrate this awareness through the use of a consistent eye-level vantage point. The authors of these perspectives have considered what life will be at street level and the "liveable" qualities are communicated clearly. In one view, certain historical buildings have been transformed to new use, and lush landscape is integrated into the design. Here, too, retail elements contribute to the vibrancy of these places within networks of pedestrian friendly streets. While larger building components are being demonstrably integrated in a good way as well, they are not the driver of the plan.

The Four Villages proposal avoids the simplistic approach—in which a series of tall buildings are seem-

ingly thrown onto a site and then camouflaged with landscape elements. The Four Villages is very much the other way around: first considering how people move around the city, experience the city, then proposing refurbishment here, new connections there, and only then adding new program. The well-considered experience of the design—the retention of the existing village structures with the new construction and new towers—was presented in such a believable way. The new elements were proposed so sensitively that they credibly did not detract from the existing retained streetscapes. There is a believable modesty to the simple language of buildings that all the renderings depict that adds to the richness of the combinations of old and new, water elements and planted components. One of the things that distinguishes this particular master plan project as opposed to some of the other ones is the attentiveness to the human scale: a more inviting and intimate scale communicated initially by the plan itself and then reinforced by the character and detail of the images.

This urban design collage method employed here compels a desire to experience the place. In this sense, the Four Villages design is a very encouraging example of a big firm operating at an international level but demonstrating responsiveness in a very intelligent way to create quality for people. However, there is a caution implicit in this recognition of such quality, intimacy, and sensitivity. The proposal for this project is a very promising start to what will surely be a long process on a large site, over a number of years. As with all immense master plans, the real challenge lies ahead: fulfilling the promise of this proposal will now entail how the development mechanisms work and how the architecture of this place is really delivered, how many developers are involved and how many architects are involved—how will this place grow over time? The proposal provides a clear image and clear qualities desired for the end result, but this is a site that is so expansive that people might well live here for generations and potentially still be living on a building site. It will be important to learn how the Four Villages design will be rolled out in practice, so that from day one quality takes precedence.

**Poly-International Plaza**
Beijing, China

If it is possible to characterize a building as a classic SOM project—in the way in the world has come to respect SOM's reputation during the last fifty years—this building has that characteristic, even emblematic, quality. The design demonstrates the practice's great strength in deriving a highly sophisticated form through the search for an innovative or dynamic high-rise structure. The jury was struck by the clarity of the structural solution: a simple answer yielding a very elegant building with a faceted curtain wall. The project succeeds as a very well-scaled, well-composed set of thirty-story "tall" volumes—importantly, not "super-tall," but rather a tall building, artistically considered.

There are several towers in the selection of the jury; the typology is the one most often associated with the reputation of SOM. The project traces back through the tradition of SOM structures such as the John Hancock Center or the Sears (now Willis) Tower, but it also pushes that tradition further by means of a highly complex interior—with vertical atriums with the top three floors designated for the owner of the building.

As SOM becomes an increasingly international presence, it is important and instructional to study where the towers are situated and how they are integrated in their host cities. This tower is interesting from the context perspective, located at a difficult and interesting intersection between two heavily trafficked motorways, in a rapidly developing capital city area. The siting and setting of the tower into the park as a free-standing object in the landscape is a "classic" approach, direct but also well-considered, and very suitable both in the location and in the relationship to the structure itself.

The project's approach—three towers instead of one mega-structure—is distinctive, creating an interesting dialogue between these three components on the site, but the design also seeks to minimize the footprint of each individual volume and gives productive consideration to the meeting of the volume with the ground plane, with a fine regard for the approach to the building and the entrance lobbies. The siting of such high-rise towers is always an important aspect; this site plays in favor of this tower because it's a place where a lively urban setting

with a lot of outdoor life is not expected. But the well-designed lobby and interstitial space in the façade work well at this intersection of two motorways.

The tower's layered "skin" creates an interim space in the outer shell with some depth; this creates opportunities for people to connect visually and physically with the buildings at the ground level. The use of the interstitial space between the outer wall and the inner skin is a good use of that façade treatment. The project's structural purity and skillful building envelope, producing such a rich visual result, and alternating between daytime reflectivity and nighttime illumination, connects abstractly to themes of cultural resonance in its Beijing and China setting. Viewing the faceted structure of these oval volumes in the cityscape will be quite an extraordinary experience, even in the changing Beijing light, perhaps especially in that light.

This building represents the epitome of SOM structural ambitions and architecture: the result of such thoughtfulness and sensitivity is a beautiful building. The British sculptor Richard Deacon once talked about the best quality of his own work; in his judgment that quality was its "rightness." In so many ways this high-rise feels right: the project is the right object in the skyline, neither overwrought nor overdone nor projecting too much of itself onto the city, but rather fitting well into the city because of its design qualities. The presentations produce an immediate sensation that this is the right solution for the site, and the right solution for the purpose; this "rightness" constitutes a major factor for beauty in architecture.

**United States Air Force Academy**
**Center for Character and Leadership Development**
Colorado Springs, Colorado

The SOM-designed Air Force Academy was an exemplary project from the start, and this project for the CCLD only carries on the successful collaboration. Uniquely, SOM was able to go back some sixty years later and work on a campus that they originally developed. To see how SOM has understood its own architecture is an encouraging sign in the firm's contemporary practice. SOM had the opportunity to create a second landmark at the Air Force Academy to complement and support its now-iconic chapel.

The design's formal volumes and imagery—shaped to point towards Polaris, the North Star—resembles aircraft motifs in forms that obviously suit the academy. The architectural idea and purpose of the honor room situated below the oculus is impressive: to continuously remind a cadet at the academy of the honor code. Once the intention of this room is understood it becomes unforgettable.

Any initial skepticism about the overt symbolic character of the design is gradually persuaded by the thoughtfulness and sensitivity of the formal language, material choices, and choreographed experience. The symbolism of the Air Force Academy is in evidence, and yes, there's a film set-like quality to the honor board room under the North Star. But the smaller details of the project are as compelling as the larger elements of the design. The entry to this part of the building, the means of descent from the platform, the entry into the different rooms and the sunken courtyards, and the experience of being inside the forum has an unparalleled architectural strength. Altogether this could be a very intense, meaningful experience, with the focus on traditions and truth resulting in progressive forward thinking for the good of the institution.

The designers have really tried to understand the soldier, the public visitor, the cadet, the person who may be convicted—their paths and perceptions—and have drawn up a series of thresholds for each. These thresholds go to the root of what architecture and planning and designing our world is about; they have addressed these thresholds as important interfaces. The aesthetics clearly utilize an SOM vocabulary. In this era and in modern architecture, military establishments are often associated with eighteenth-century structures; in this project there is an interest in creating a dialogue about how the military should engage with contemporary culture. This powerful addition represents a transformation from a sense of duty and patriotism based on faith towards one based on reason.

# *SOM Journal* 8
# Submissions

850-Bed Medical City
Abu Dhabi, United Arab Emirates

Al Hamra Firdous Tower
Kuwait City, Kuwait

Alliance New Country Village
Nanhu, Jiaxing, China

Dancing Line

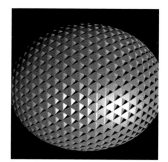

Desert Arena
Abu Dhabi, United Arab Emirates

Enabling Iterations

King Abdullah City for Atomic and
Renewable Energy
Saudi Arabia

Kuwait University Administration Facilities
Shadadiya, Kuwait

The Ledge at Skydeck Chicago
Chicago, Illinois

Shenzhen Gangxia Parcel #1
Shenzhen, China

Tanjong Pagar
Singapore

The Tree Trunk Towers

Baietan Area Urban Design Master Plan
Central Guangzhou, China

Balihai: A Blue City
Tianjin-Binhai Region, China

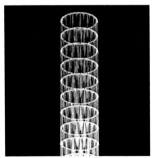

Creating Simplicity

Goldsun Hangzhou
Hangzhou, China

Istanbul Tower
Istanbul, Turkey

Jiangsu Wujiang Tower
Wujiang, China

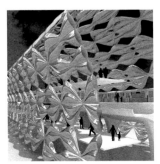

Midway Airport
Chicago, Illinois

The New School University Center
New York, New York

PS0: Net Zero Energy School
Staten Island, New York

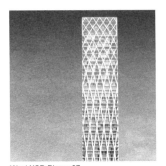

Wuxi XSD Phase 07
Wuxi, China

19

# 1 New Blackfriars
# London, United Kingdom
## Designed 2011

London's relationship to the river Thames is defined in many locations by public space, public buildings, landmarks, or by cultural activities. In the west a cluster of these buildings exists around the South Bank, the Houses of Parliament, and Tate Britain. Similarly, in the east, the public spaces around Canary Wharf and the emerging public space around the O2 Arena form another recognizable cluster. There are more such "urban events" elsewhere in the city, but through a history of commercial development facing the water, the cohesiveness of this pattern has been lost.

The 1 New Blackfriars development grows from a single geometry, one which has carved central landscaped avenues on the ground plane to maximize views and daylight to the apartments. The project's unique geometry allows the site to be subtly modified by weaving pedestrian and visual connections together with the client's programmatic requirements. The landscaped avenues increase permeability across the site, opening up the site to the neighborhood and providing a perceived continuity with Tate Modern and public waterfront. The architectural solution is reminiscent to the scale and character found in Shad Thames and the London dockland fabric. The tight-knit neighborhood will benefit from linked residential, cultural, retail, and office environments, encouraging a strong sense of community.

The tower's signature tapered form creates a strong presence within its urban context and carefully mediates the waterfront. It further reinforces its relationship to the area with its main pedestrian approach via the railway arches and through a path connecting Blackfriars train station to the south.

Internally the tower offers awe-inspiring panoramic views of London, providing residential and commercial tenants a stimulating live-work environment. A unique series of flexible unit types was created for the development. They can be interchanged and refined during design development; to be flexible and to be able to react to market conditions and the client brief. For greater efficiency, the corners of the residential buildings were identified as the ideal location for the innovative "one-and-a-half loft" configuration—one-and-a-half story apartments stacked into three story bundles, allowing some of the loft units to achieve an added half story of internal height. It also allows several single story studios to be sandwiched between. By increasing the living spaces from three to four-and-a-half meters, the unit type improves on other new residential developments in London.

The façade of 1 New Blackfriars is designed to enhance views and maximize natural light, while protecting the buildings from solar gain. The façade is a quilted, high-performance skin that creates a dappled pattern of shadows. The external envelope is articulated on a modular grid of stone panels to enhance city and waterfront views. Every module is rotated on the vertical axis and tilted in such a way to filter light, creating an ever-changing interplay of light and shadow. On the east, west, and south façades, the glass panels are deliberately rotated in such a way to dramatically reduce solar gains and radiation.

The roof is designed as a triangulated network of sequential green, semi-green, and brown landscapes. With direct access from the elevator cores, the lower roof terrace is expected to be the most popular among tenants. This area is designed as the greenest component of the landscape sequence, providing communal seating areas and terraces for everyday use by residents. The landscaped roof contributes to the project's aspirations for restoring ecology and providing biodiversity, and to support thermal insulation and rainwater reclamation.

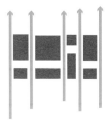 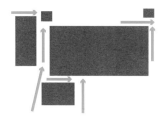 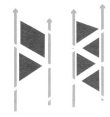

1862: When London was the trading center of the world, the Thames was the focus of economic and trading activity. Due to the importance of the Thames the city fabric directed towards its riverbanks.

Today: By the turn of the century, all trade activity on the Thames relocated to the docklands in east London and the city transformed its relationship with the Thames allowing its edges to be privatized and dominated by industry.

Future: The concept for the development reconnects the Thames back to the surrounding neighborhoods by weaving key transportation hubs, cultural institutions and pedestrian routes through the 1 New Blackfriars site.

2

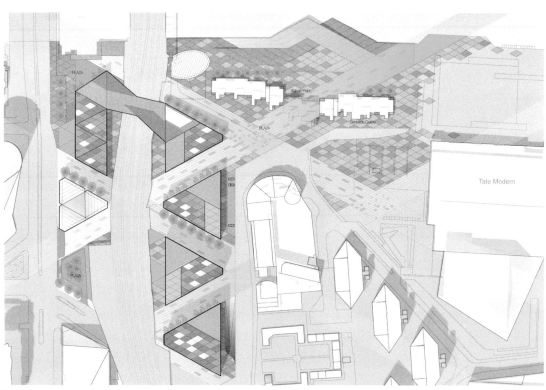

3

<1 Aerial view of London showing site
 2 Weave concept
 3 Weave diagram with buildings showing
   relationship to Tate Modern
 4 Aerial view over site

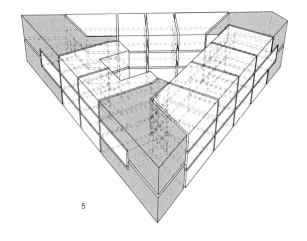

5

5 Residential floor stacking diagram
6 One-and-a-half-height loft evolution
7 Program diagram
8 Typical level residential floor plans

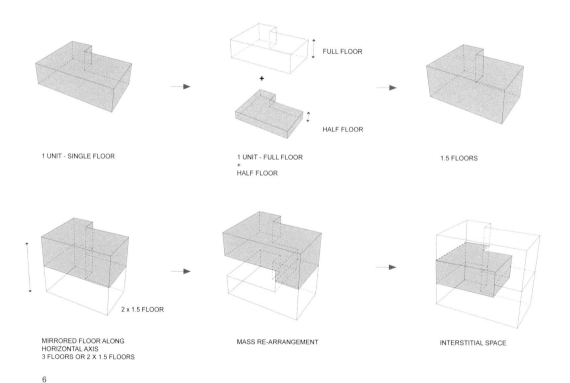

1 UNIT - SINGLE FLOOR

FULL FLOOR

+

HALF FLOOR

1 UNIT - FULL FLOOR
+
HALF FLOOR

1.5 FLOORS

2 x 1.5 FLOOR

MIRRORED FLOOR ALONG
HORIZONTAL AXIS
3 FLOORS OR 2 X 1.5 FLOORS

MASS RE-ARRANGEMENT

INTERSTITIAL SPACE

6

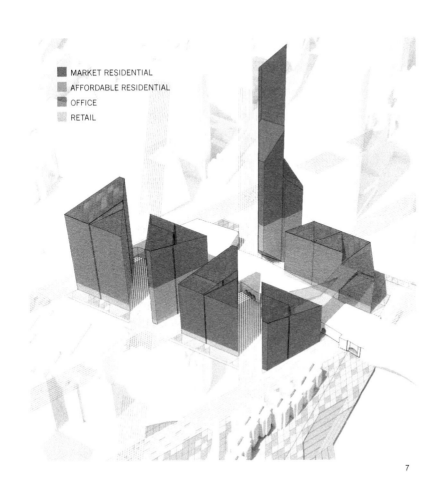

MARKET RESIDENTIAL
AFFORDABLE RESIDENTIAL
OFFICE
RETAIL

7

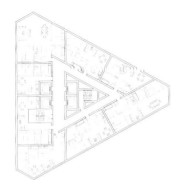

8

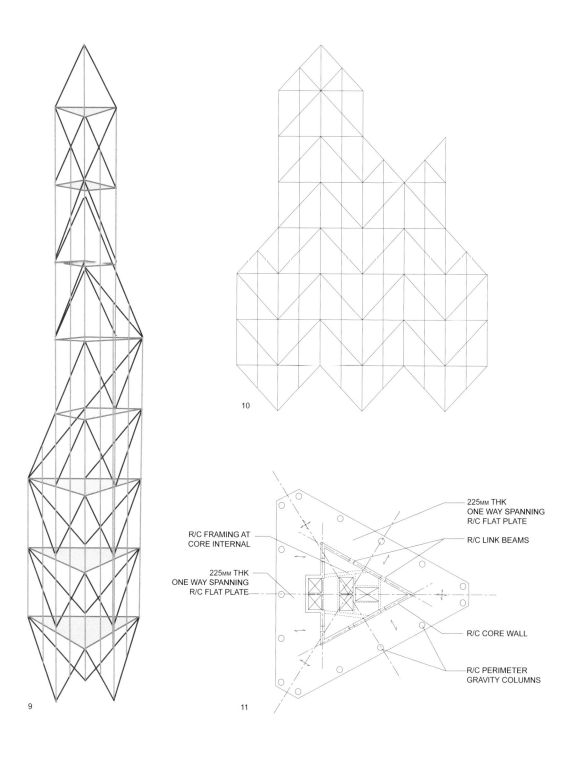

R/C FRAMING AT
CORE INTERNAL

225мм THK
ONE WAY SPANNING
R/C FLAT PLATE

225мм THK
ONE WAY SPANNING
R/C FLAT PLATE

R/C LINK BEAMS

R/C CORE WALL

R/C PERIMETER
GRAVITY COLUMNS

9

10

11

9 Steel structure concept diagram
10 Exploded structural concept elevation
11 Structural plan diagram
12 Transverse section

12

# Seoul Light DMC Tower
## Seoul, South Korea
## Designed 2009–11

Seoul Light DMC Tower is a mixed-use project envisioned as a new model in sustainable super-tall building design. Located north of the Han River on the western edge of Seoul, Seoul Light DMC Tower acts as a gateway to the city. As approached from Incheon Airport and points west, the tower will be a visitor's first impression of Seoul as a global city. The project symbolizes South Korea's continued economic growth and support for sustainability as a necessary component of urban development. The tower represents a shift towards a performance driven model of super-tall design. At 2,100 feet (640 meters) tall, the tower will be the tallest building in East Asia when it is completed.

The architectural expression of Seoul Light DMC Tower reinforces sustainability strategies at the core of its design. The tower is shaped through gently curving arcs and smooth transitions between the main north-south and east-west façades. Mega-columns along the perimeter reinforce the expression of the mass and provide a natural break to a series of solar louvers. On the east and western façades, a pattern of both horizontal and vertical fins act as a shield against early- and late-day sun, while horizontal shades on the southern face shield the interior from high afternoon sun, thereby reducing internal cooling loads. Solar photovoltaic panels are integrated into specific zones of the louvers most affected by the sun, generating additional renewable energy. The tower's soaring crown collects and channels natural light deep into the lower portions of the tower, giving a connection to the outdoors and reducing demands on artificial lighting.

A large central void and two perimeter voids are carved through the upper half of the tower, creating another opportunity to collect natural light and clean air, and to generate renewable energy by capitalizing on the principles of a solar updraft tower within the tall vertical central void. The design calls for six vertical axis wind turbines at the crown of the tower to be driven by the air as it is drawn out of the void; as the buoyant air rises, the air flow draws in cool, fresh air from below, which also drives wind turbines at the base of the building. The inner panels of glass that line the central void are designed with materials that catch, reflect, and hold light, which reduces the reliance on artificial light. An active phyto-remediation green wall is planted within the perimeter voids to clean and replenish the internal air supply. Radiant cooling through chilled beams, radiant floor heating, and the drawing of tempered air through green atriums adds further efficiency. A gray water reclamation tank within the tower drastically reduces the dependence on the public water supply and eliminates the need for potable irrigation water. By taking advantage of naturally occurring events such as stack effect and solar radiation gain, Seoul Light DMC Tower is able to generate its own power and therefore reduce municipal energy consumption to a fraction of typical levels. At the core of SOM's scheme is an integrated sustainability strategy that uses the natural physics of tall buildings in order to generate power. Through the use of the stack effect and wind turbines located at the top of the building, almost three percent of the building's energy consumption is self-generated from clean, renewable sources.

At the base, an eight-story retail podium connects the tower to the surrounding urban fabric and encourages pedestrian flow through the site between the Digital Media City business district to the north and the recently rehabilitated Nanji public park to the south.

< 1  Aerial view of site
  2  Aerial rendering of tower
  3  Site plan
  4  Plaza level rendering

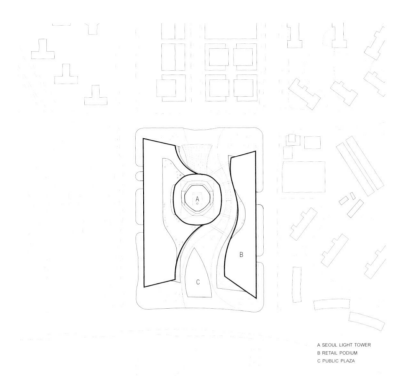

A SEOUL LIGHT TOWER
B RETAIL PODIUM
C PUBLIC PLAZA

120 ft
40 m

3

4

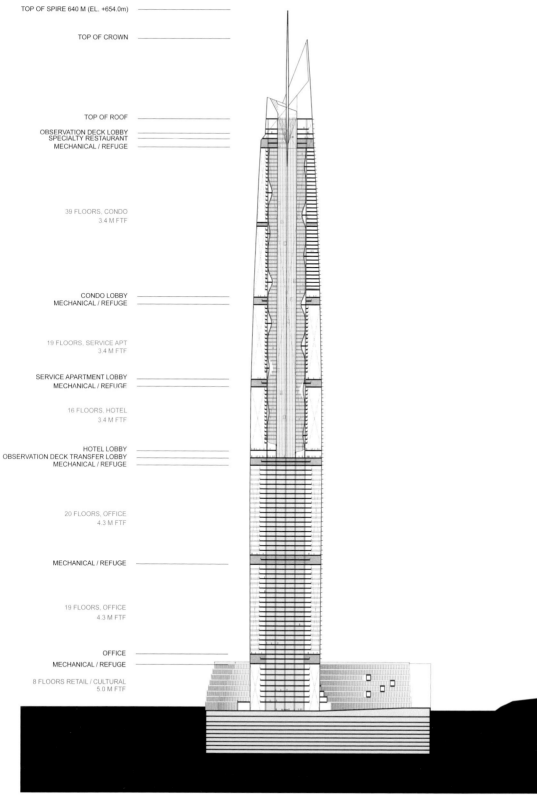

TOP OF SPIRE 640 M (EL. +654.0m)

TOP OF CROWN

TOP OF ROOF

OBSERVATION DECK LOBBY
SPECIALTY RESTAURANT
MECHANICAL / REFUGE

39 FLOORS, CONDO
3.4 M FTF

CONDO LOBBY
MECHANICAL / REFUGE

19 FLOORS, SERVICE APT
3.4 M FTF

SERVICE APARTMENT LOBBY
MECHANICAL / REFUGE

16 FLOORS, HOTEL
3.4 M FTF

HOTEL LOBBY
OBSERVATION DECK TRANSFER LOBBY
MECHANICAL / REFUGE

20 FLOORS, OFFICE
4.3 M FTF

MECHANICAL / REFUGE

19 FLOORS, OFFICE
4.3 M FTF

OFFICE
MECHANICAL / REFUGE

8 FLOORS RETAIL / CULTURAL
5.0 M FTF

5

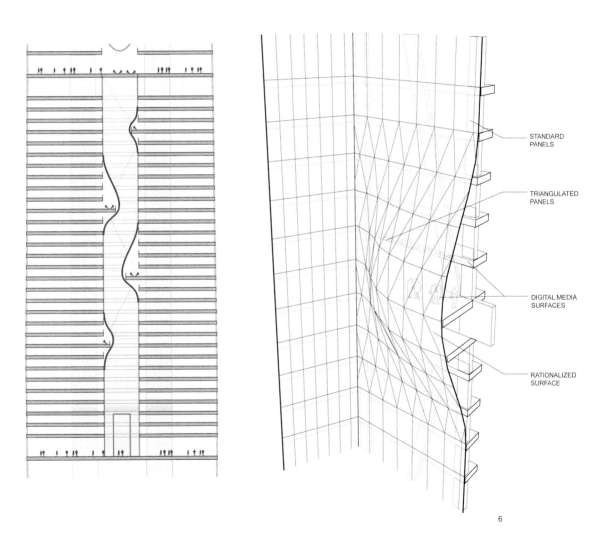

STANDARD
PANELS

TRIANGULATED
PANELS

DIGITAL MEDIA
SURFACES

RATIONALIZED
SURFACE

6

5  Building section
6  Central void amenity enclosure diagram

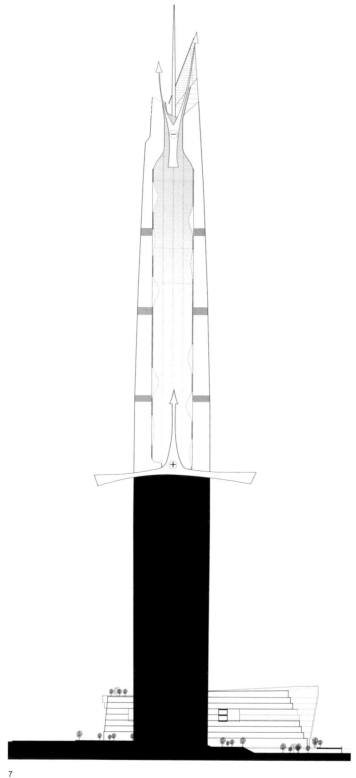

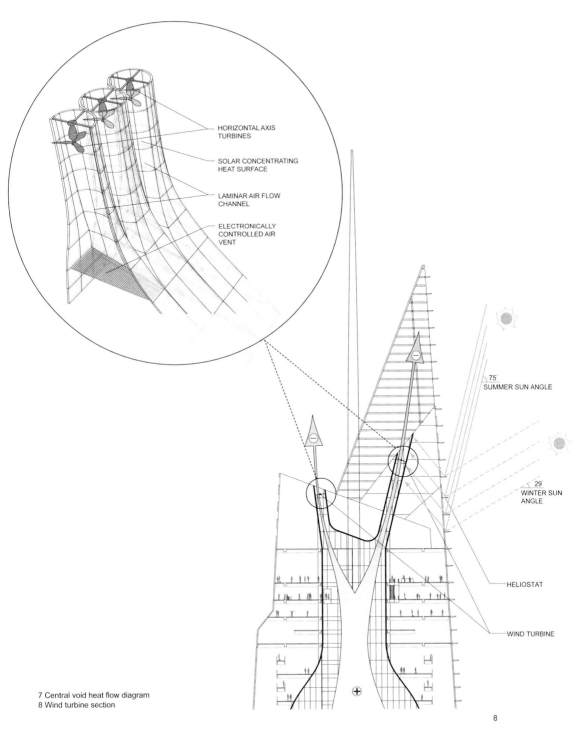

HORIZONTAL AXIS
TURBINES

SOLAR CONCENTRATING
HEAT SURFACE

LAMINAR AIR FLOW
CHANNEL

ELECTRONICALLY
CONTROLLED AIR
VENT

75
SUMMER SUN ANGLE

29
WINTER SUN
ANGLE

HELIOSTAT

WIND TURBINE

7 Central void heat flow diagram
8 Wind turbine section

8

# BASELINE BUILDING ENERGY USE 100%

| | |
|---|---|
| RADIANT FLOOR HEATING FOR HOTEL AND RESIDENCES | 3% ↓ |
| RADIANT COOLING AND CHILLED BEAM SYSTEM FOR OFFICES | 4% ↓ |
| HIGH-PERFORMANCE GLAZING AND SHADING | 4% ↓ |
| HIGH-EFFICIENCY OFFICE AND RESIDENTAIL EQUIPMENT | 4% ↓ |
| HIGH-EFFICIENCY LIGHTING | 5% ↓ |
| HELIOSTAT & DAYLIGHT CONTROLS | 3% ↓ |
| OCCUPANCY CONTROLS | 1% ↓ |
| CENTRAL VOID HEAT RECOVERY | 2% ↓ |
| NATURAL VENTILATION | 5% ↓ |
| HIGH-EFFICIENCY HEATING/COOLING PLANT | 6% ↓ |
| ENERGY RECOVERY | 3% ↓ |
| DEMAND BASED VENTILATION | 2% ↓ |
| ON-SITE POWER HEAT RECOVERY | 4% ↓ |
| INTEGRATED PHOTOVOLTAICS | 2% |
| WIND TURBINE GENERATORS | 3% |
| MICROTURBINE ON-SITE POWER GENERATION | 15% |
| WIND TURBINES AND METHANE RECLAMATION | 20% |
| ENERGY USE | 14% |

**BASELINE BUILDING ENERGY USE REDUCED BY 86%**

46% REDUCTION

20% REDUCTION

20% REDUCTION

20% ON-SITE GENERATION

UP TO 20% NEAR-SITE GENERATION

9  Energy use chart
10 Detail photograph of AMPS green wall
11 Rendering of green wall within central void
12 Air exchange diagram
13 Floor plans showing green wall locations
14 AMPS green wall air exchange

9

10

11

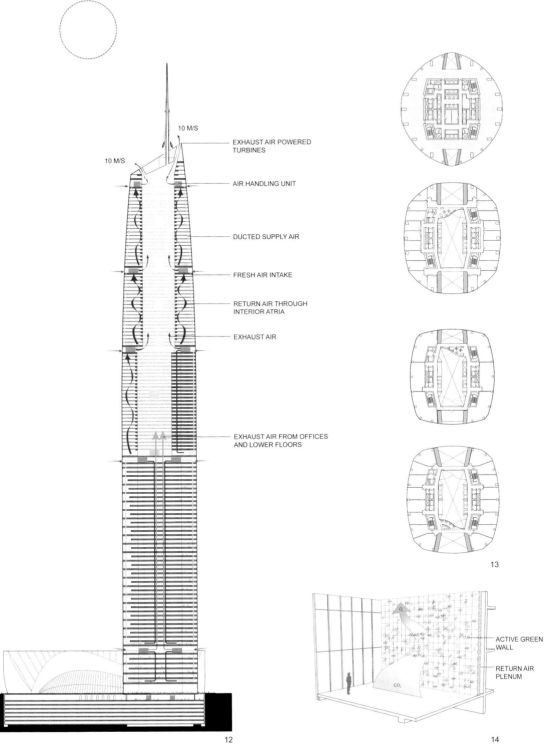

EXHAUST AIR POWERED
TURBINES

10 M/S

10 M/S

AIR HANDLING UNIT

DUCTED SUPPLY AIR

FRESH AIR INTAKE

RETURN AIR THROUGH
INTERIOR ATRIA

EXHAUST AIR

EXHAUST AIR FROM OFFICES
AND LOWER FLOORS

13

ACTIVE GREEN
WALL

RETURN AIR
PLENUM

12

14

37

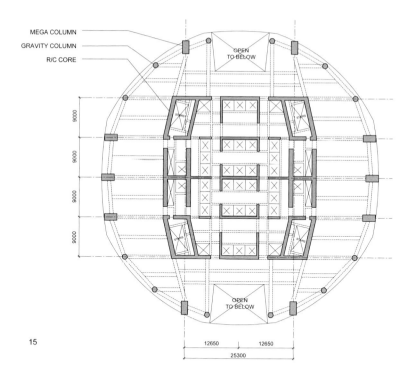

MEGA COLUMN
GRAVITY COLUMN
R/C CORE

OPEN TO BELOW

OPEN TO BELOW

9000
9000
9000
9000

15

12650    12650
25300

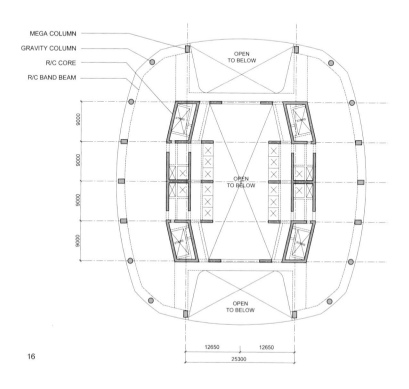

MEGA COLUMN
GRAVITY COLUMN
R/C CORE
R/C BAND BEAM

OPEN TO BELOW

OPEN TO BELOW

OPEN TO BELOW

9000
9000
9000

16

12650    12650
25300

15 Typical one-way beam and slab floor framing
16 Typical flat slab with band beam floor framing
17 Structural system

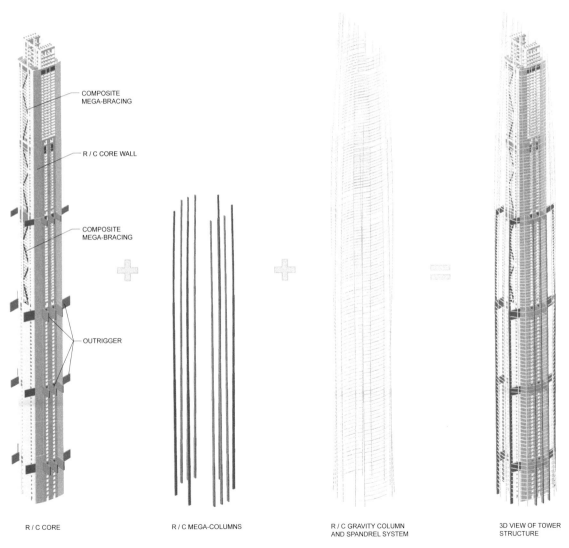

COMPOSITE
MEGA-BRACING

R / C CORE WALL

COMPOSITE
MEGA-BRACING

OUTRIGGER

R / C CORE

R / C MEGA-COLUMNS

R / C GRAVITY COLUMN
AND SPANDREL SYSTEM

3D VIEW OF TOWER
STRUCTURE

17

# King Abdullah Financial District Conference Center

Riyadh, Saudi Arabia

Designed 2011

The new conference center in the King Abdullah Financial District in Riyadh, Saudi Arabia, is designed as an extension of the rugged desert landscape: its organic profile and faceted skin stitch together the building and the adjacent terrain. The center incorporates a planted "xeriscape" roof to protect a suite of auditoriums and multi-purpose halls from the harsh desert sun, winds, and sandstorms. On the building's interior, the space between the angular roof surface and the more rectilinear box-like conferencing facilities defines a network of gathering and temporary exhibition areas that are naturally illuminated by sunlight filtering through the exterior skin. During the design process, solar radiation levels on the building form were analyzed to gain an understanding of surfaces where there was less direct sun, which in turn determined locations and density of glazing. Conversely, fully glazed roof areas at peaks in the building form harness the power of the desert sun by drawing its heat into solar absorption panels. The resulting super-heated panel causes thermal convection of the air near the ceiling surface, driving air from common areas out through vents in the roof. This air movement permits the main circulation spaces to be ventilated naturally in the temperate months, and to extract waste air without mechanical fans during the hottest months, when water circulating through the floor slabs will provide cooling to building occupants. Sensors in the building skin monitor temperature, rain, and sand storm activities, and control the roof vents accordingly.

The center is based on a concept of flexible conferencing, providing a multipurpose event hall with operable walls, a six-hundred-seat auditorium with lecture and cinema support, and a "digital forum" that allows all venues to be internally and externally networked. The conference rooms are designed as immersive four-wall video environments, with walls that contain retractable projection screens that allow users to conduct virtual video meetings with the center's other conference rooms or remote locations worldwide. The conference rooms are clad in electrochromic glass which can be changed from clear to opaque to control light levels and privacy. A "media cloud" in the ceiling of each conference room will have the ability to communicate with attendees' mobile media devices, permitting wireless sharing and projection of user content in a meeting setting. Dynamic interactive displays allow conference organizers to control signage for individual rooms and conference venues, and elevators are equipped with video screens that carry event information and other conference-related content.

The building's structural framing system forms a light triangulated lattice with three layers: the primary mega-frame which defines the major facets, a secondary dia-grid that connects to the midpoints of the mega-frame, and a tertiary exterior wall mullion system that carries the glazing units, insulated glass fiber reinforced concrete panels, and the planted panels containing native desert grasses. Conventional soil in the planted panels was deemed to be too heavy and impractical for the sloping roof geometries, so the design team developed an artificial growth medium called "hypertufa," which derives its name from porous desert limestone that wicks irrigation moisture to the plants and allows roots to attach to the medium's small pores.

1 600 SEAT AUDITORIUM
2 750 SEAT EVENT HALL
3 PREFUNCTION SPACE
4 GREAT HALL
5 CAFE
6 CONFERENCE ROOMS
7 MONORAIL STATION
8 SKYWALK BRIDGES

100 m
250 ft

2

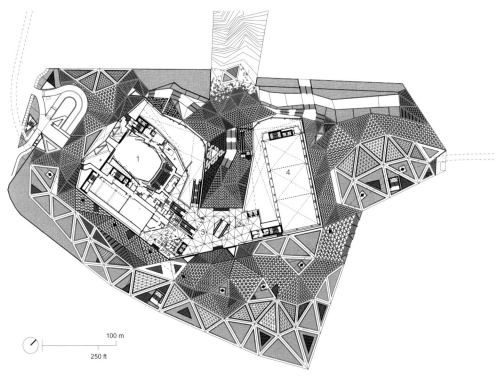

100 m
250 ft

3

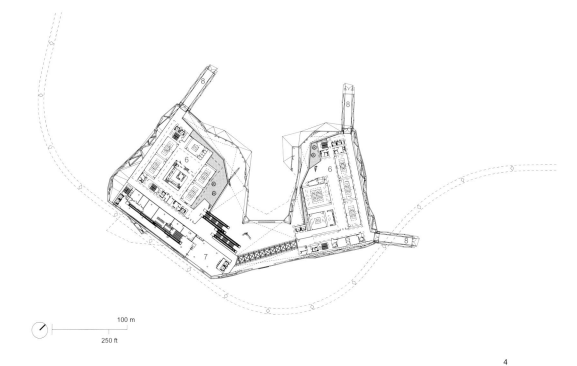

100 m
250 ft

4

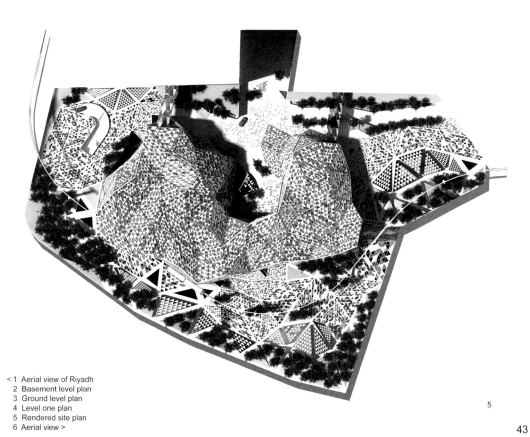

< 1  Aerial view of Riyadh
  2  Basement level plan
  3  Ground level plan
  4  Level one plan
  5  Rendered site plan
  6  Aerial view >

5

43

7

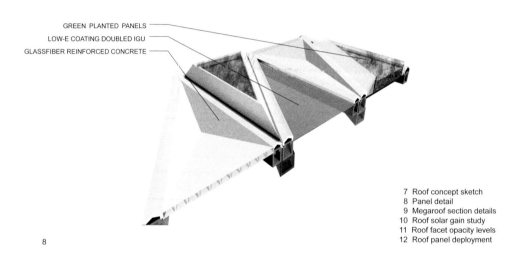

GREEN PLANTED PANELS
LOW-E COATING DOUBLED IGU
GLASSFIBER REINFORCED CONCRETE

8

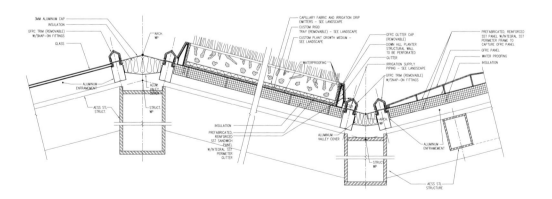

9

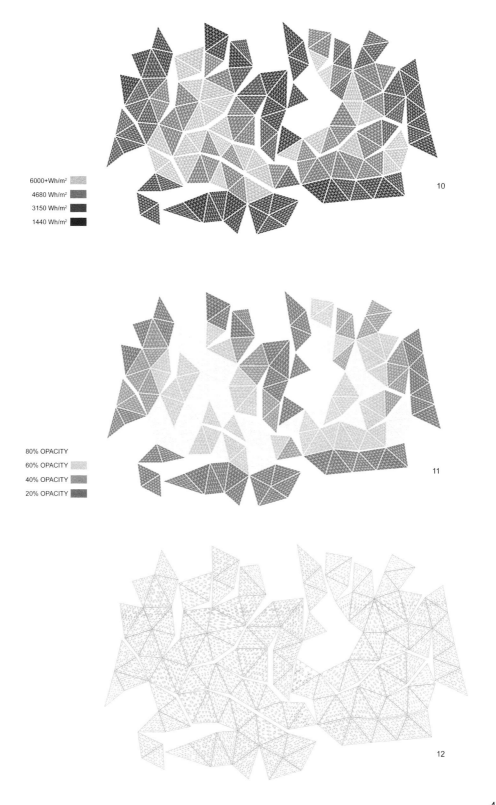

6000+Wh/m²
4680 Wh/m²
3150 Wh/m²
1440 Wh/m²

10

80% OPACITY
60% OPACITY
40% OPACITY
20% OPACITY

11

12

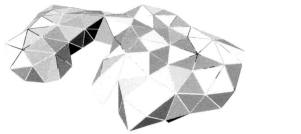

3.15 SQ M

.50 SQ M

GREEN PLANTER AREA TEST

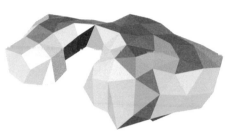
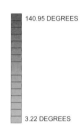

140.95 DEGREES

3.22 DEGREES

FACET ANGLE TEST

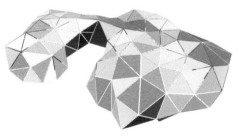
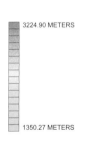

3224.90 METERS

1350.27 METERS

MAXIMUM GLASS EDGE LENGTH TEST

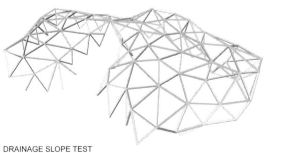

1.73 DEGREES

173.51 DEGREES

DRAINAGE SLOPE TEST

13

14

13 Panel optimization tests
14 Great hall
15 Event hall pre-function

15

16

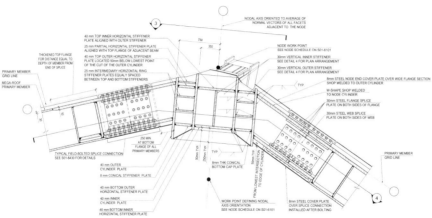

NODAL AXIS ORIENTED TO AVERAGE OF
NORMAL VECTORS OF ALL FACETS
ADJACENT TO THE NODE

40 mm TOP INNER HORIZONTAL STIFFENER
PLATE ALIGNED WITH OUTER STIFFENER

25 mm PARTIAL HORIZONTAL STIFFENER PLATE
ALIGNED WITH TOP FLANGE OF ADJACENT BEAM

40 mm TOP OUTER HORIZONTAL STIFFENER
PLATE LOCATED 50mm BELOW LOWEST POINT
OF THE CUT OF THE OUTER CYLINDER

THICKENED TOP FLANGE
FOR DISTANCE EQUAL TO
DEPTH OF MEMBER FROM
END OF SPLICE

25 mm INTERMEDIARY HORIZONTAL RING
STIFFENER PLATES EQUALLY SPACED
BETWEEN TOP AND BOTTOM STIFFENERS

PRIMARY MEMBER
GRID LINE

MEGA-ROOF
PRIMARY MEMBER

NODE WORK POINT
SEE NODE SCHEDULE ON S01-6101

30mm VERTICAL INNER STIFFENER
SEE DETAIL 4 FOR PLAN ARRANGEMENT

30mm VERTICAL OUTER STIFFENER
SEE DETAIL 4 FOR PLAN ARRANGEMENT

8mm STEEL NODE END COVER PLATE OVER WIDE FLANGE SECTION
SHOP WELDED TO OUTER CYLINDER

W-SHAPE SHOP WELDED
TO NODE CYLINDER

30mm STEEL FLANGE SPLICE
PLATE ON BOTH SIDES OF FLANGE

30mm STEEL WEB SPLICE
PLATE ON BOTH SIDES OF WEB

TYPICAL FIELD-BOLTED SPLICE CONNECTION
SEE S01-6430 FOR DETAILS

250 MIN.
AT BOTTOM
FLANGE OF ALL
PRIMARY MEMBERS

40 mm OUTER
CYLINDER PLATE

8 mm CONICAL STIFFENER PLATE

8mm THK CONICAL
BOTTOM CAP PLATE

40 mm BOTTOM OUTER
HORIZONTAL STIFFENER PLATE

40 mm INNER
CYLINDER PLATE

40 mm BOTTOM INNER
HORIZONTAL STIFFENER PLATE

WORK POINT DEFINING NODAL
AXIS ORIENTATION
SEE NODE SCHEDULE ON S01-6101

PRIMARY MEMBER
GRID LINE

8mm STEEL COVER PLATE
OVER SPLICE CONNECTION
INSTALLED AFTER BOLTING

17

18

16  Construction progress photo
17  Section through structural node
18  Construction progress photo
19  Construction progress photo
20  Structural stress analysis
21  Construction progress photo

19

Beam Disp: D (XYZ) (mm)

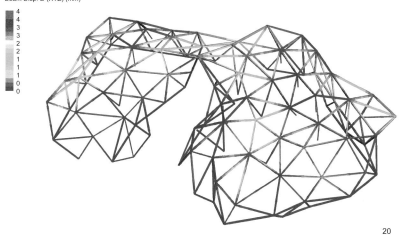

20

# The Planning of Four Villages on University Island

## Guangzhou, China
## Designed 2008–09

Explosive, high-density development at a scale and pace previously unknown in human history is destroying integrity of place in the world's fastest growing regions. As the population sprints past the 7 billion mark and growth is concentrated in and around cities, human-scale design and livability are becoming increasingly rare. SOM's urban design integrating four Pearl River villages and the University Island in the Panyu district of Guangzhou—where the villages have survived for centuries—is an innovation that can help humanize future eruptive developments in China and other radically growing urban habitats throughout the world.

The scale and speed of University Island's growth is scarcely imaginable. In just seven years, an agricultural island was transformed into seven campuses in the Jeffersonian vein, housing 400,000 university freshmen, faculty, and staff. This cluster of campuses was so dispersed that the students were effectively confined to their rooms, with no on-campus or near-campus amenities or natural escapes.

The four ancient farm villages that survived relocation after the massive build-out were isolated pockets with virtually no interaction with the new influx of Pearl River islanders. Those villages and their people were the last island vestiges of the ancient civilization of South China. Regional and local officials were well aware that island growth had come at an unbearably high cultural cost, and had commissioned earlier urban planning attempts to mitigate a massive fait accompli. They asked SOM's global urban design practice to come in and see what could be done.

A city design team from SOM met with their new government clients, toured the campuses, and walked the four villages that had grown organically and were shaped by social consensus over the course of generations. Architecturally, the villages were created in a classic Lingnan style, which the SOM team—headed by Director Douglas Voigt—saw was not so much a design approach as a way of life. The Lingnan style arranges the built and the natural environments in a plain, harmonious simplicity for daily ease of living, enriched by its combination of garden and city characteristics.

SOM designers initiated an in-depth dialogue with the villagers about the very actions that had kept the island's unique integrity of place alive. The villagers keenly understood what the planners were after and provided key principles needed to restore the island's identity and sense of place.

In the Guangzhou University Villages case, a new idea of preservation was created and the large campuses' spaces in between were woven together and humanized by modern urban design principles derived from traditional techniques—with each iteration of the design process being critiqued by a group of engaged villagers.

The plan's organizing framework for redevelopment was to retain and integrate historic buildings, pathways, waterways, and landscapes, clustering taller developments to act as "hills" that rose up from and out of the more historic areas, while creating a cohesive new sense of identity across University Island. The plan proscribed humanizing the previously stark isolation of campus living by creating new retail and commercial centers with walkable streets and connected pedestrian pathways, to bring livability and diversified quality of life within a short walk of each campus and each village.

The traditional Lingnan approach is a well-balanced synergy of traditional development patterns and natural systems. Explosive growth usually results in anything but a healthy balance of the built and the natural. Fundamental to SOM's Guangzhou University Villages plan is restoration of a healthy relationship between people and nature. Its vision for University Island is a place of great parks and quality open spaces, of modern canals and restored ecosystems, and a place that uses less water than any other district of Panyu City, by using natural infrastructures that clean and return water to the soil.

This SOM urban design project was community building at high density and with a large population already in place when the designers began their work. Through dialogue and community consensus, a new methodology resulted in integrating the past with new and forward-thinking strategies shaped by sensitivity to nature, human needs, and high performance design. The students and faculty are happy—with convenient places to go and things to do—the villagers are respected and more prosperous.

2

< 1  Existing Suishi Village lotus pond
  2  Project location and its relationship to
     major urban centers
  3  Four villages (in blue), roads, and location of
     surrounding universities:
     (a) Sun Yat-Sen University
     (b) Guangdong University for Foreign Studies
     (c) Guangzhou University of Chinese Medicine
     (d) Guangdong Pharmaceutical University
     (e) South China University of Technology
     (f) Guangdong University of Technology
     (g) Guangzhou Academy of Fine Arts
     (h) Guangzhou University
     (i) South China University
     (j) Xinghai Conservatory of Music
  4  Images of present day Suishi Village

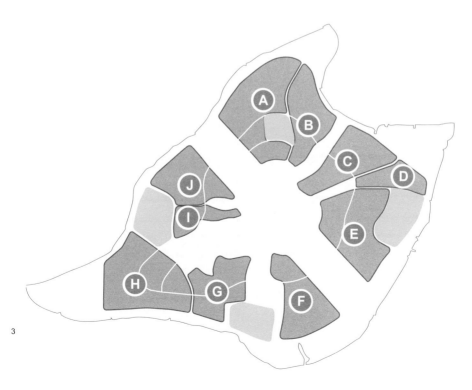

3

5

5 Aerial view of four villages on University Island:
  A: Beigang Village
  B: Suishi Village
  C: Nanting Village
  D: Beiting Village

6

7

8

9

6  Rendering of proposed Beigang Village. Beigang Village has
   emerged as a vibrant urban village centrally located between
   multiple student housing areas
7  Rendering of proposed Suishi Village plan. Suishi Village is
   organized around a linked series of existing ponds that have
   been restored as the center for village life
8  Rendering of proposed Nanting Village plan. For residents
   of Nanting Village, new schools will be located in a park-
   like setting that extends from the existing hill and natural
   landscape
9  Rendering of proposed Beiting Village plan. Located at an
   important entry point to the island, Beiting Village provides
   a new identity and skyline that will welcome visitors to the
   island

10 Aerial view of Suishi Village today
11 Urban design plan and proposed uses

10

CIVIC AND EVENT SPACE
ACTIVE OPEN SPACE
HERITAGE BUILDINGS
PEDESTRIAN PATH

11

# Poly International Plaza

Beijing, China
Designed 2010–12

Located approximately half way between the Forbidden City and Beijing Capital Airport, the Poly International Plaza will occupy a prominent position adjacent to the Capital Airport Expressway and its interchange with the Fifth Ring Road. The area is a former village which is rapidly becoming engulfed by Beijing's relentless expansion. This project will be the first building in a proposed new business district. For now, the site is a flat, open expanse without streets or infrastructure. An emerging district of hundred-meter-tall residential buildings is rising approximately half a kilometer to the west, an open space reserve is to the east, a major public open space is planned immediately to the west and south, and an unorganized agricultural-industrial sprawl characterizes the area to the north. Surrounded by open space on three sides, and with its proximity to a major arrival point to the city, the project will be a highly visible terminus to the new district's proposed skyline.

The proposal is for a speculative office building of sixty thousand square meters that seeks to compete in the marketplace by providing a unique, high-quality work environment, in contrast to the typical indifferent flexible lease space becoming ubiquitous throughout China. The client will occupy the topmost three floors with their own offices. The proposal creates a unique light-filled spatial experience for entering and moving through an office building, utilizes a long-span structural strategy to open up interior spaces, and employs a highly sustainable architectural/mechanical approach to address the climatic and air quality issues particular to Beijing.

A faceted exoskeleton system is a part of the primary structure for the building, forming an outer envelope which sleeves over an elongated core and a pair of arc-shaped office spaces. The office spaces are further enclosed within a second interior envelope of glazing. The space between the inner and outer envelopes creates opportunities for social interactions and offers physical and visual connectivity between floors. Mechanically, the semi-climatized interstitial space mediates exterior temperature extremes, reducing the overall building energy consumption by twenty-three percent and carbon emissions by eighteen percent.

At the narrow ends of the building the interstitial space expands to create two distinct atriums which open outward to admit daylight and direct views toward central Beijing to the southwest and the airport to the northeast. Embedded within the atriums are a series of communicating stairs, shared meeting rooms, and an expressed, fritted-glass low-rise elevator tower with glass cabs to the south. At the upper floors, the mid-rise and high-rise elevator lobbies open directly towards the atriums affording immediate geographic orientation by way of external views. The atriums provide places of respite and community, protected from Beijing's cold winters, hot summers, and days of poor air quality.

The structural exoskeletal diagrid system creates an open, column-free work environment. With spans between diagrid nodes of approximately eighteen meters, views from the interior will be expansive. In order to maintain primarily axial loads in the elliptical form, diagrid members are constructed from straight, rather than curving segments. Floor framing loads are transferred to the diagrid at primary diagrid nodes only. Thus, every second floor frames directly into the exoskeleton, while the intervening floors are supported by hangers from the floor immediately above. The outer layer of glazing is the result of mapping a surface directly onto the straight structural members, generating a faceted rather than elliptical form. The varying reflections created by these surfaces (rather than shadows) will ensure legibility of the form in Beijing's typically dim, diffused light.

<< 1 Aerial view of site
< 2 Rendering of view from highway
3 Building composite
4 Typical level plan
5 Site plan

OVERALL FACETED FORM

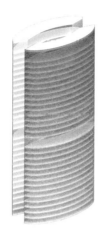

TYPICAL OFFICE LEASE DEPTH
OF 11M AREA

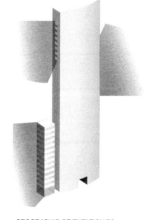

GEOGRAPHIC ORIENTATION TO
EXTERIOR THROUGH ATRIUMS
FROM ELEVATOR LOBBIES

SUBTRACTED END CONDITIONS ALLOW
INSERTION OF SOCIAL INTERACTION SPACES

AXIAL LOAD DISTRIBUTION ALLOWS
COLUMN FREE INTERIOR AND ATRIUMS

BUILDING COMPOSITE

3

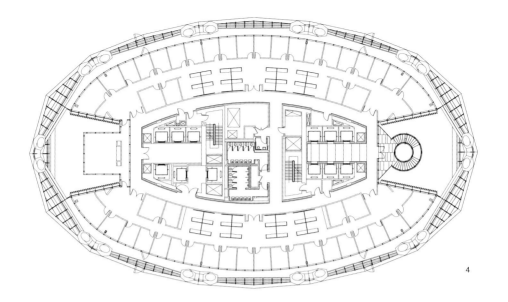

4

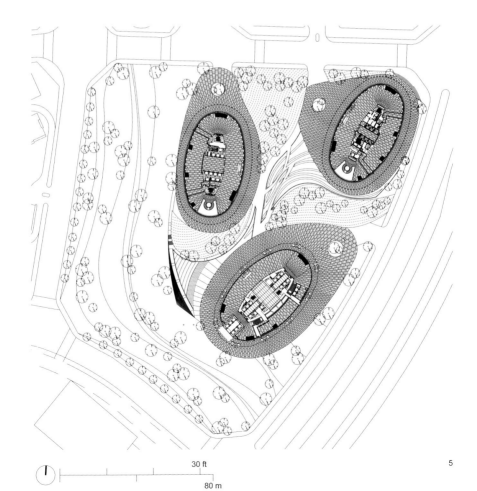

5

30 ft

80 m

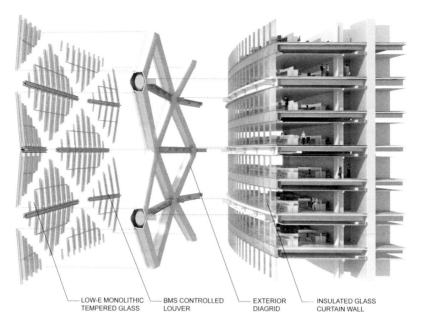

LOW-E MONOLITHIC  BMS CONTROLLED   EXTERIOR     INSULATED GLASS
TEMPERED GLASS   LOUVER          DIAGRID      CURTAIN WALL

6

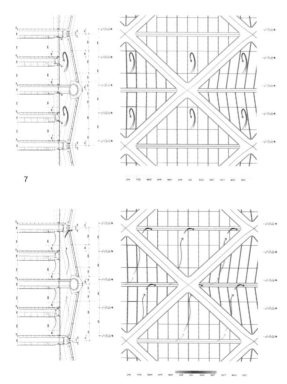

6 Exploded components diagram
7 Open horizontal operable louvers section
  and detail during winter months
8 Closed horizontal operable louvers section
  and detail during summer months
9 Sectional perspective

7

8

9

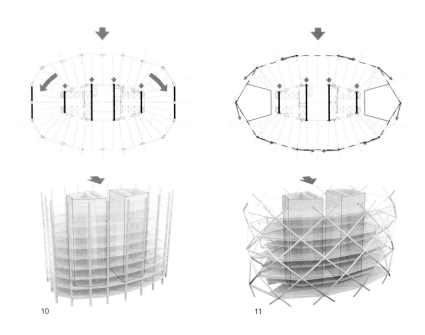

10    11

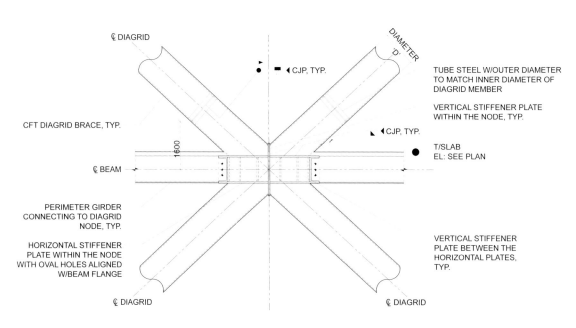

℄ DIAGRID

DIAMETER 'D'

▶
●  ▬  ◀ CJP, TYP.

TUBE STEEL W/OUTER DIAMETER
TO MATCH INNER DIAMETER OF
DIAGRID MEMBER

VERTICAL STIFFENER PLATE
WITHIN THE NODE, TYP.

CFT DIAGRID BRACE, TYP.

◣ ◀ CJP, TYP.

1600

℄ BEAM

● T/SLAB
EL: SEE PLAN

PERIMETER GIRDER
CONNECTING TO DIAGRID
NODE, TYP.

HORIZONTAL STIFFENER
PLATE WITHIN THE NODE
WITH OVAL HOLES ALIGNED
W/BEAM FLANGE

℄ DIAGRID

VERTICAL STIFFENER
PLATE BETWEEN THE
HORIZONTAL PLATES,
TYP.

℄ DIAGRID

12

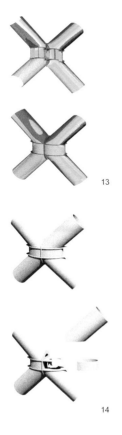

13

14

15

16

17

# United States Air Force Academy Center for Character and Leadership Development

## Colorado Springs, Colorado

## Designed 2010–12

In 1954 SOM was selected to design a campus for the newly created United States Air Force Academy, set for a picturesque site abutting the Rocky Mountains. In contrast to this rugged backdrop, SOM created a rigorously modern campus with an iconic chapel at its center, the entirety of which has since been designated a National Historic Landmark District.

Recently the Air Force Academy created a new program, the Center for Character and Leadership Development (CCLD), a new building for which they imagine as a reason-based design in counterpoint to the Academy's iconic (faith-based) chapel. Presented with a unique opportunity to revisit one of its most significant projects fifty years later, SOM was asked how to design a new building that defers to the chapel and the discipline of the Academy's planning grid, while also asserting itself within the campus.

SOM designed a building that creates a precise optical alignment with the North Star. The CCLD uses the North Star, Polaris, to symbolize its core values and illustrates this idea by placing Polaris at the focal point of the CCLD's emblem. Setting forth a design that makes Polaris its focal point with a 105-foot-high skylight structure, SOM created a powerful landmark which embodies the mission of the CCLD.

Symbolically placed at the building's heart, the Honor Board Room is where investigations into potential violations of the Cadet Honor Code take place. Relative to the CCLD, Polaris is located due north at thirty-nine degrees altitude regardless of season or time of day; and a cadet respondent seated inside the Honor Board Room is precisely aligned with Polaris through openings in the ceiling and the top of the skylight. These openings—elliptical in plan, but circular when viewed at thirty-nine degrees—are calibrated to encompass the small circular yearly track of Polaris for centuries to come.

Below the skylight structure and at the center of the CCLD is the Forum, a flexible and dynamic gathering space for academic and social interaction. Its terraced levels accommodate gatherings of a variety of scales and formality from casual interaction in soft seating to formal lectures and symposia. Surrounding the Forum are glass-walled break-out rooms, further increasing the flexibility of the Forum and the transparency of the main level.

With this meeting place at its center, the CCLD negotiates a critical meeting point between the secure precinct of the cadets and the unsecure precinct of the public. It acts as a nexus, weaving together the public, cadets, professors, and visiting VIPs, and connects to the surrounding buildings with multiple entrances, each identifiable by a threshold of glass and light.

Among the CCLD's leadership goals is leadership in sustainability. As a demonstration of that ambition, the building will achieve LEED Platinum certification. SOM has approached sustainability through the lens of integrated building systems which influence all parts of the building's design, construction, and operation. Chief among many sustainable strategies is an energy efficient approach to climate control which utilizes earth tubes, high-efficiency air handling units, the solar chimney effect within the skylight structure, and radiant heating and cooling. Additionally, abundant natural light is available through the skylight structure as well as floor-to-ceiling glass abutting gardens. It is tempered by high-performance glazing and supplemented with optimized artificial lighting. Finally, part of the building's energy requirements are offset by onsite renewable energy generation in the form of a photovoltaic array.

2

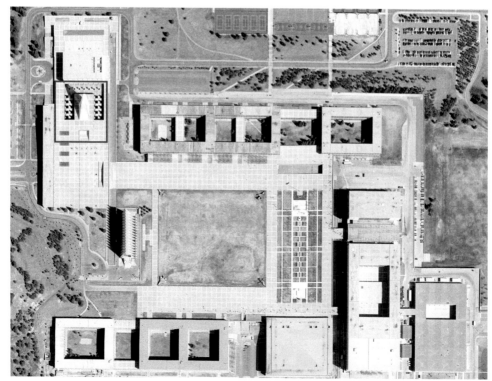

3

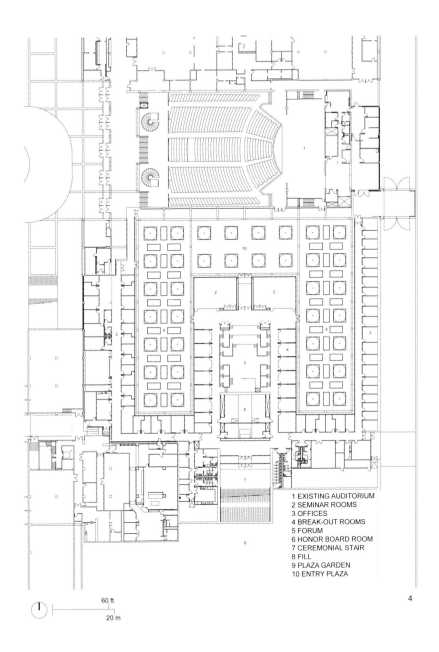

1 EXISTING AUDITORIUM
2 SEMINAR ROOMS
3 OFFICES
4 BREAK-OUT ROOMS
5 FORUM
6 HONOR BOARD ROOM
7 CEREMONIAL STAIR
8 FILL
9 PLAZA GARDEN
10 ENTRY PLAZA

60 ft
20 m

4

< 1  Cadet Campus, 1962
  2  Cadet chapel: a faith-based icon
  3  Aerial view of campus
  4  Ground level plan

5 Model section view
6 Site model

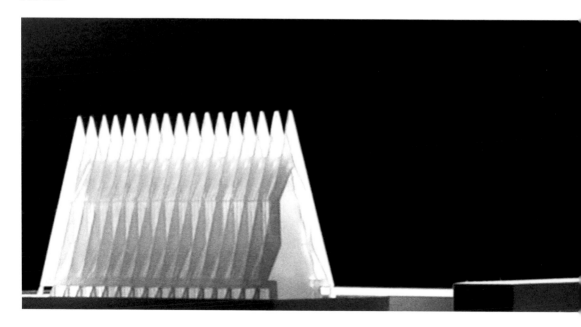

5

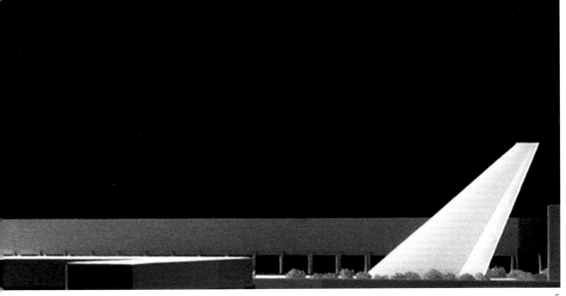

6

7 The Forum
8 View looking north

9

9 Skylight structure
10 Honor Board Room
11 Structural concept: Lateral loads imposed on the diagrid are resisted by structural members that taper
toward the center of the span where the loads are
greatest. The resultant gradient of curving profiles
is a visual representation of the most efficient structural solution.
12 Skylight structural support
13 Sustainability features >
14 Aerial view >>

10

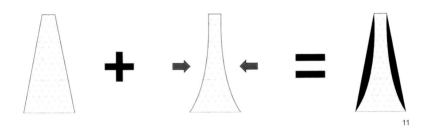

11

12

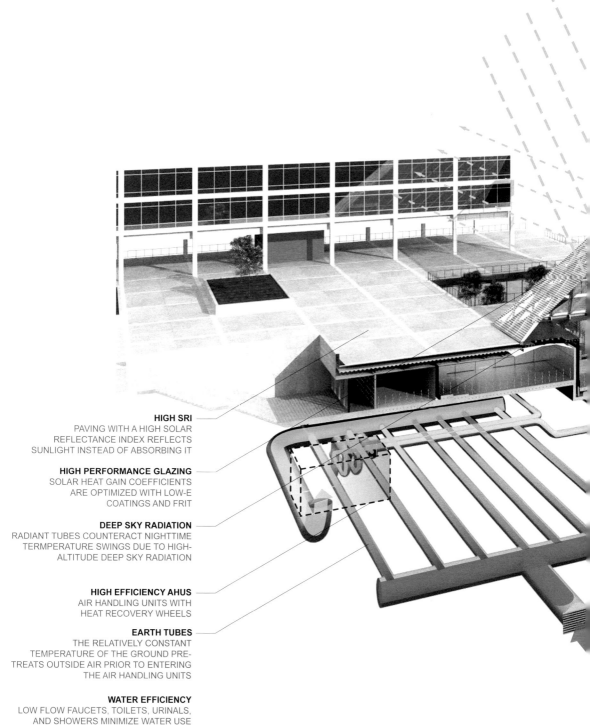

**HIGH SRI**
PAVING WITH A HIGH SOLAR
REFLECTANCE INDEX REFLECTS
SUNLIGHT INSTEAD OF ABSORBING IT

**HIGH PERFORMANCE GLAZING**
SOLAR HEAT GAIN COEFFICIENTS
ARE OPTIMIZED WITH LOW-E
COATINGS AND FRIT

**DEEP SKY RADIATION**
RADIANT TUBES COUNTERACT NIGHTTIME
TERMPERATURE SWINGS DUE TO HIGH-
ALTITUDE DEEP SKY RADIATION

**HIGH EFFICIENCY AHUS**
AIR HANDLING UNITS WITH
HEAT RECOVERY WHEELS

**EARTH TUBES**
THE RELATIVELY CONSTANT
TEMPERATURE OF THE GROUND PRE-
TREATS OUTSIDE AIR PRIOR TO ENTERING
THE AIR HANDLING UNITS

**WATER EFFICIENCY**
LOW FLOW FAUCETS, TOILETS, URINALS,
AND SHOWERS MINIMIZE WATER USE

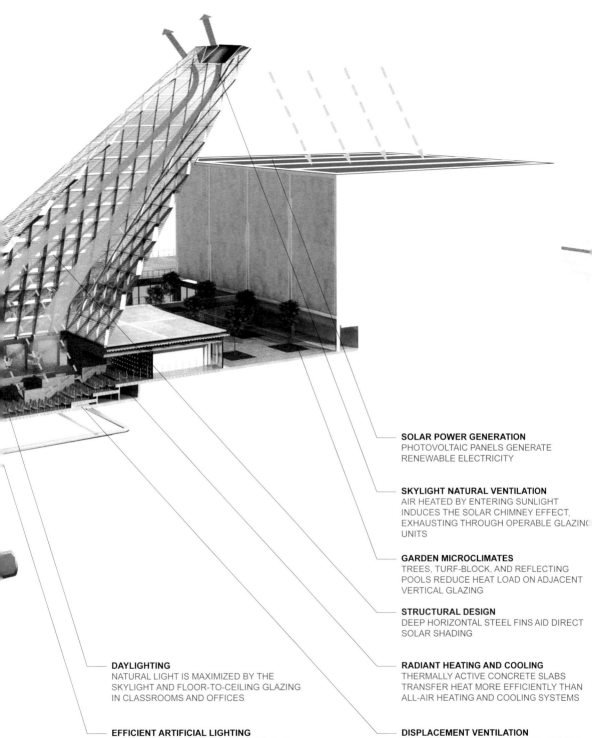

**SOLAR POWER GENERATION**
PHOTOVOLTAIC PANELS GENERATE
RENEWABLE ELECTRICITY

**SKYLIGHT NATURAL VENTILATION**
AIR HEATED BY ENTERING SUNLIGHT
INDUCES THE SOLAR CHIMNEY EFFECT,
EXHAUSTING THROUGH OPERABLE GLAZING
UNITS

**GARDEN MICROCLIMATES**
TREES, TURF-BLOCK, AND REFLECTING
POOLS REDUCE HEAT LOAD ON ADJACENT
VERTICAL GLAZING

**STRUCTURAL DESIGN**
DEEP HORIZONTAL STEEL FINS AID DIRECT
SOLAR SHADING

**RADIANT HEATING AND COOLING**
THERMALLY ACTIVE CONCRETE SLABS
TRANSFER HEAT MORE EFFICIENTLY THAN
ALL-AIR HEATING AND COOLING SYSTEMS

**DAYLIGHTING**
NATURAL LIGHT IS MAXIMIZED BY THE
SKYLIGHT AND FLOOR-TO-CEILING GLAZING
IN CLASSROOMS AND OFFICES

**EFFICIENT ARTIFICIAL LIGHTING**
ENERGY EFFICIENT FIXTURES, DAYLIGHT
SENSORS, OCCUPANCY SENSORS,
MOTORIZED SHADES

**DISPLACEMENT VENTILATION**
 100% OUTSIDE AIR IS DELIVERED AT LOW
SPEEDS NEAR THE FLOOR

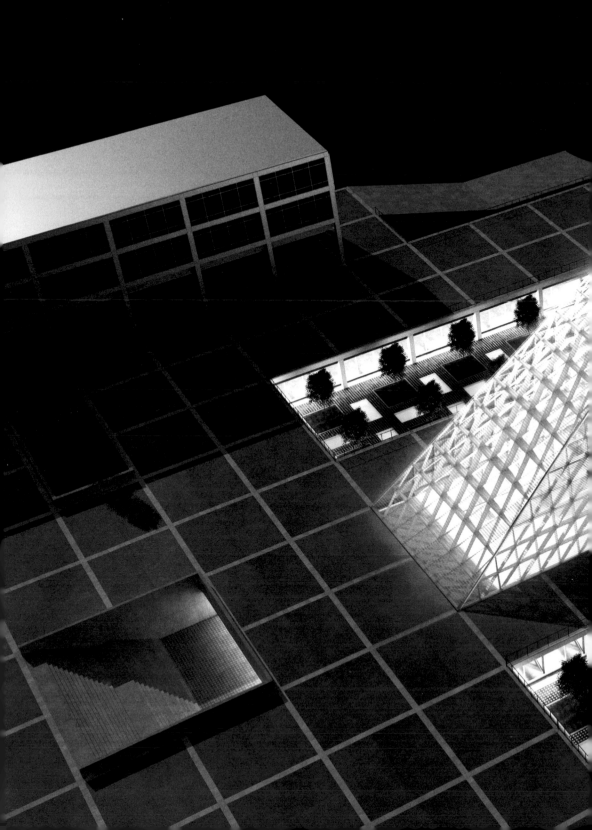

*Metropolis* magazine cover, October 2004

# Design in the Collaboration Era

## Susan Szenasy

The Seattle Central Library opened on Sunday, May 23, 2004. We knew that every media outlet would make it a story about the great man, Rem Koolhaas, its genius architect. We also knew—and for some time had been thinking about how to approach the subject—that such projects are much more complex than one man's story, no matter how dynamic, articulate, and skilled that one man might be. And, of course, Koolhaas is all of those things. But what we wanted to figure out was how to tell the story of collaborations at every phase and in every area of the project. And we knew, as our senior editor at the time, Karen Steen, wrote, that "even a book-length work wouldn't do the process justice."

Realizing the limitations of the magazine format (in 2004 we could splurge nineteen pages plus the cover on this story while in 2012 we would be happy with ten), our editors identified the essential collaborators on the project. Starting with the research team that defined the library's needs in the electronic age, as well as its intensely involved public (there's a lot of rain in Seattle which makes for a well-read populace), their findings informed the design every step of the way. It was found that the librarians themselves needed to be in close contact with their visitors. As a consequence, the design team took the librarians out of their offices and put them on the floor giving each person a small GPS-connected electronic device called Vocera, through which they could share their expert knowledge with the curious public.

Computer specialists were consulted on ways to make the library's unique information navigation system an intuitive process for users of varying skills. Engineers, on a larger scale, worked out the building's distinctive façade. In fact, it took three teams to make the mesh glass pattern work: Arup, Magnusson Klemencic, with façade consultants Front and Dewhurst Macfarlene, and curtain-wall manufacturer Seele.

The Central Library's famous Books Spiral, the inclined, four-story walkway through the stacks, actually started life in 1999. It was then that the two architecture firms OMA and LMN began brainstorming with graphic designer Bruce Mau on how to arrange the books, while allowing for expected growth over the next twenty-five years. The design had to be flexible enough so that no single section would outgrow space allotted to it.

The interiors, key to the success of such an intensely used public space, bear the aesthetic touch of Petra Blaisse, Koolhaas's longtime collaborator. In addition to her team at OMA, the local interior designers, headed up by Sam Miller at LMN were told at the outset that all materials in the project had to pass the "three Ps" standard: pee, puke, and poop. With this in mind, the conjoined team would not be seduced by flashy objects, yet they were able to use such iconic Dutch treats as Maarten Van Severen's chairs made by Vitra and the induction lamp system (known for its 100,000-hour performance) by Phillips.

The hidden interiors, those service spaces that make the library run smoothly—like the sorting room—required the expertise of software engineers to operate a conveyor system for thousands of books, videos, CDs and DVDs, largely untouched by human hands and needing collation every hour.

When we learned that Seattle Central's window washers were recruited from the local mountain-climbing community, we knew that our story of collaboration was richer than any single tale of a high-profile architect could ever be. And so we added a special feature to our multi-layered story: the people who operate the library—security teams, mechanical operations staff, even the guy who sells newspapers around the corner—in addition to those who use it every day. All of them make the space work. They have helped make the distinguished building into a local and national destination, by word of mouth and other forms of communication.

This story could never have been told if Joshua Prince-Ramus, founding partner of Koolhaas's OMA New York, hadn't come to our offices to share information with our editorial and art staff. It is rare for this kind of sharing to happen. Architects usually talk to the press about themselves and their work, conveniently ignoring the complexity of each project and giving priority to their grand design moves. Yet everyone talks about the need to work collaboratively. What's more, the conversation about teamwork has picked up volume since building information modeling software entered the design process, changing it forever.

The changes brought about by the ever-evolving software systems have come to firms that, even a few years ago, had trouble giving credit to their interior designers, lighting designers, engineers, and landscape architects without which their practice could not exist. Despite the lack of information coming from the firms, we know that everyone collaborates. They have to. The projects today are simply too large and too complex to pull off without the expertise of many different people.

For example, the profession's embrace of sustainable design (both environmental and social) has created a need to consult with such far-flung experts as materials scientists and accessibility experts. Some firms, like HOK, which adopted biomimicry as a basis of their designs, include a biologist on their teams and they are proud to talk about this fact. Others like Perkins + Will employ materials specialists who have developed the firm's Precautionary List of chemicals known to be harmful to human health, and shares this information openly with anyone who cares to navigate the web. And Joshua Prince-Ramus, whose mother worked at the time as a civil rights attorney, consulted her on ADA (Americans with Disabilities Act) requirements while designing the ramp's incline for Seattle Central.

Once in a while some large multi-national firm will share their collaborative process at public events like the annual AIA Convention. But when they do, they tend to talk about their teaming up with local architects, the software that allowed them to communicate seamlessly across borders and cultures, and the phenomenally tight-deadlines to build whole cites on the sands of the Middle East or in some burgeoning Chinese region.

So why is collaboration so hard for architects to talk about? Why is information disclosure so meager and spotty? Is it the system of starchitects who dominated media coverage during the last decades of the twentieth century and into our own times? Is it the limitations of journalists who tend to focus on a great personality? Or is it the media that shows no taste for telling a complex

story? We're all caught in a system of communication that was designed for a different time and very different economic and cultural circumstances.

But something is changing in every architecture firm, regardless of size. The new generation of digital natives, architects who have used electronic media since they were babies, is now working. They bring with them unprecedented skills in computer-aided design, their ability to combine software programs (some made for design, some made to measure performance) is recognized universally, and their social networks connect them to others around the globe, creating vast communities of information. This fact became real for me some five years ago.

I was moderating a discussion with young interior architects and designers in San Francisco who talked about how they work, how their education has helped/or not helped them, and what the newest designers are brining to the table. The designers on the panel talked about having at least two social networks open on their computers at all times. They used these networks to research the project they were working on. Looking for a stain resistant, non-toxic, high-performing, attractive material? These designers did not rush to the firm's library, but sent out the question to their social networks. Through these networks, designers who might have seen each other as competitors, just a few years before, are now helpful allies. In essence, they are saying: You help me today. I will help you tomorrow. All of a sudden the world of collaboration has expanded beyond formerly narrow and restricting boundaries.

At just about the same time, I was doing some interviews for our second film, *Brilliant Simplicity.* My subject was designers, in practice ten or fewer years, all either winners or noteworthy runners-up in our Next Generation Design Competition, which, since 2004, has focused on research, collaboration, and the resulting innovation. When David Benjamin and Soo-in Yang of The Living took the microphone, they discussed open source, something everyone under twenty-five knows about today, and few over fifty want to acknowledge. These two professors at Columbia's Graduate School of Architecture, Planning, and Preservation talked about something they call "flash research." They spend three months or less and $1,000 or less on a timely and difficult architectural problem, such as how to make buildings breathe, post their findings on the Internet, where it's available to others working on the same problem. Open source software allows such distant and sporadic collaborations, while expanding the profession's body of knowledge and intriguing the curious public.

For that same film project, I talked to Anna Dyson who ran the Rensselear Materialab researching high performance building materials. She became known among progressive architects and their collaborators for her ability to bring many specialists together in one room to focus on particularly difficult problems in the built environment. It was her team's active solar façade that brought Dyson to our attention through the Next Generation Competition.

Her unstoppable drive to help remake hopelessly outdated building materials and practices is irresistible. It was no surprise to us when, a few years later, she became director of the Center for Architecture, Science and Ecology (CASE), embedded in the New York City offices of SOM; still the only graduate program if its kind. It focuses on the architecture sciences, technology, and built ecologies. To Dyson, collaboration is the cornerstone of the innovation that takes place there.

It's worth reminding ourselves of the case CASE makes for the necessity for collaboration: "Buildings account for over a third of the total energy consumption in the United States. As new construction projects increase exponentially in global economies, acceleration in the pace of architectural innovation and the implementation of sustainable material and energy technology becomes ever more urgent." To address these urgent issues, Dyson brings together experts, many non-architects, whose knowledge is essential to the breakthrough solutions we need in times of severe climate change. In fact, she says, these professionals who may be experts in hydrogels among other things, don't put the same limits on solving a problem as architects do. As a result, her experience in working with diverse teams is an eye-opening process that most architects have yet to experience.

I have been taking *Brilliant Simplicity* into architecture offices and to mixed groups of designers all over the country for several years now. Before the recession hit, very few wanted to talk about collaboration and innovation. They were too busy on too many projects. Then the construction industry fell off the cliff, taking some sixty thousand architects and related design professionals with it. Now as the profession tries to rebuild itself, every-

Breathing wall, Living City, mock-up

one is looking for new ways to approach design in the twenty-first century, which arrived with a bang in 2008 as the market crashed.

We talk about the necessity to innovate, knowing that without research and teamwork, with everyone at the top of his or her game, innovation can't happen. We talk about open source, still an alien concept to the senior members of the firms, while the young designers smile in the back of the room. We talk about ways practitioners can team up with local universities, focusing on mutually beneficial research projects, that address the problems created by global warming, shrinking resources, and aging populations. Everyone is in a discovery mode.

As a blogger from our POV column sums up today's profession:

> We are now immersed, once again, in a period of unbridled technological innovation—this time not by the analog (the Machine Age) but by the digital (the Information Age). And while the analog era required great skill specialization to engineer, create, produce, and operate physical things, the digital era demands an integrated approach to create and manage parametric

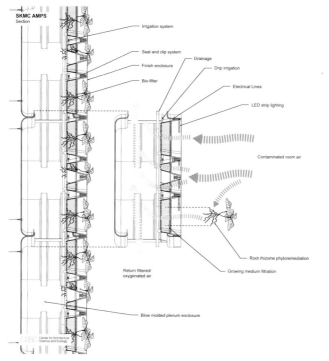

SKMC AMPS Section

*processes* (economics, planning, design, and engineering) that directly feed and, in fact, physically control *outputs* (fabrication and construction). In other words, cross-disciplinary thinking is an emerging prerequisite to success. Lest you think this is the stuff of dreams—that architecture will always require the same foundation skill sets that made our fathers (well, my architect father, anyhow) successful, and that this new digital era is simply a fad—you need to look no further than to our newest group of employees, Generation Y (aka the Millennial or Net Generation).

They are the first generation to grow up with digital ubiquity. Armed with unparalleled access to both information and one another, they don't recognize the boundaries that have defined our profession until now, and are accordingly pioneering a transformation of architecture, not just in its digitally-enabled physical form but in its creative and managerial *processes*. They write scripts to analyze zoning, economics, construction scheduling, and environmental influences to inform decision-making empirically. They crowd-source clients and communities to harness the collective intelligence and establish highest-value needs. They write programs to coordinate directly between 3D modeling software and robotic construction machines. And they aren't afraid to leave the security of long-term employment and forge their own paths, focusing their integrated skills on redefining what it means to create and inhabit the built world.[1]

Clearly, we are entering a new and different, and for some very difficult, phase in the practice of architecture. Some say the profession has become "irrelevant" as everyone on the team, from subcontractor to furniture manufacturer, works with the same software, leaving design as a minor interruption in the proceedings. Others are more proactive, looking for a redefinition of architecture. And those who enlist bright young people will have the advantage. From them we can all learn new ways to collaborate, new ideas about connecting with others, new ways of finding relevant information, and new approaches to making junior designers key members of their teams. That's how the true age of collaboration is starting to shape up.

1   http://www.metropolismag.com/pov/20120604/the-built-environment-v-3-0#more-24682

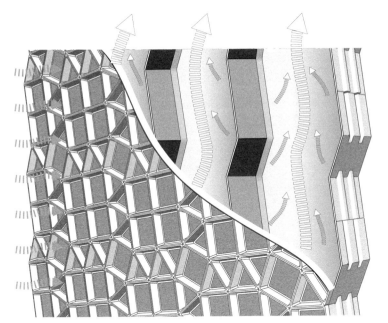

## DUCTED AMPS BIO-FILTER WALL

AMPS duct enclosure allows the system components to be packaged in stackable modular units. These units can then be tesselated to act as a series of vertical ducts that draw air through the growing media and return filtered air vertically. This produces a series of free flowing columns of air that can be drawn by fan power. The growing media cassettes, irrigation, and drainage plug into the face of the duct enclosure allowing for free air movement behind. A series of trim rings seal the face of the system and contain LED grow lighting for the plants.

AMPS Bio-filter wall diagram showing return air through vertical duct enclosures at bottom, and return filtered or oxygenated air at top

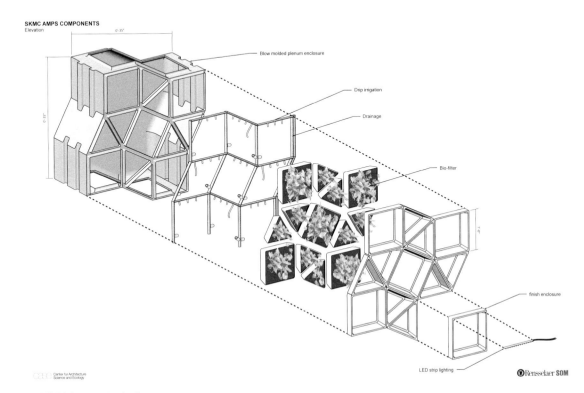

SKMC AMPS Components, elevation

SOM, Single family houses, Oak Ridge, TN, 1949. (Hedrich-Blessing, Chicago Historical Society)

# Teamwork after CIAM: Team 10 at Royaumont
## Eric Mumford

Hovering over the field of architecture is the specter of the lone genius artist-architect, the willful designer who claims all of the credit and often maligns the contributions of others. For many, these attributes correlate closely to the perceptions of some of the heroes of modern architecture, notably Frank Lloyd Wright and Le Corbusier. At the same time, the field often celebrates teamwork, both in the design and programming phases, and by necessity in the construction process. There have been many efforts to resolve this seeming contradiction, and the fate of these efforts, in around 1960, of the Team 10 group to work collectively provide a sobering example of the challenges involved.

Team 10's efforts took place in the very different practice environment of the mid-twentieth century, when the tension between individual genius and teamwork had been identified by Henry-Russell Hitchcock in 1947. Hitchcock emphasized the importance of Detroit industrial architect Albert Kahn's office in setting a pattern for modern architectural practices where "the strength of the firm . . . depends not on the architectural genius of one man . . . but in the organizational genius which can establish a fool-proof system of rapid and complete plan production."[1] The goal of such a system was the "perfect mutual coordination as machine parts come from the various sections of the factory," which were then combined into a finished product on the final assembly line.

Hitchcock drew parallels between "Albert Kahn, Inc." and the Tennessee Valley Authority (TVA)—"another great architectural bureaucracy." The TVA had given form to the visions of the Regional Planning Association of America (RPAA) for decentralized regional organizations that combined new hydroelectric powered industry with suburban and rural living. Hitchcock saw this kind of architectural and urban development bureaucracy reach a new level of organization of production with the design of Oak Ridge, Tennessee. Largely planned between 1943 and 1949 by the recently established SOM,[2] Oak Ridge was a new city of 75,000 defense workers,

organized around the making of the first atomic bomb. Against the skilled bureaucratic architectural efforts of Albert Kahn, SOM, and other firms, which foreshadowed the future of the field after the war, Hitchcock set the example of Wright's Guggenheim Museum (1943–59), which he described as "the architecture of genius." Unlike bureaucratic designs based on "the sum of their particular amenities," this kind of architecture depended on its overall impact, much like poetry and painting. Even if the galleries were not completely successful (as was the case at the Guggenheim), it was the essential artistic concept, developed by a particular name architect, that mattered.[3]

Although this postwar tension between bureaucracy and genius was already foreshadowed in the nineteen-twenties during debates between Le Corbusier and German socialist advocates of Neues Bauen (for example, Hannes Meyer), the way that the debate unfolded in the nineteen-fifties was quite contrary to earlier modernist aspirations. This became clear to the members of CIAM (Congrès internationaux d'architecture moderne/International Congresses of Modern Architecture), as the group's postwar efforts to further direct new urban patterns began to seem somewhat feebly situated between the vigor of occasional members who had become recognized modern genius-architect figures (Ludwig Mies van der Rohe, Alvar Aalto, Oscar Niemeyer, Marcel Breuer, and others), and utilitarian, often highrise, housing production by large government authorities. This split situation, exemplified in the postwar polarization between the Museum of Modern Art's canonization of certain modern architects and Robert Moses's massive New York housing and infrastructural efforts, which made no use of their talents, created serious challenges for the field. As the architectural schools, press, and exhibition venues became transfixed by genius designers of various persuasions, housing and urbanism in both Western industrial cities and the rapidly decolonizing postwar world shifted to the edges of the profession's concerns, rather than being at the center, as had been the case before the war.

It was the effort to respond to this new challenge that prompted the formation of Team 10, an unanticipated outcome of the efforts by the CIAM leadership to hand over the organization to a few hand-picked youth members. Led by Le Corbusier, they chose Georges Candilis, Jacob Bakema, and Aldo van Eyck to prepare future congresses.[4] At CIAM 9, held in Aix-en-Provence in 1953, and intended to develop a new "Charter of Habitat" to guide what had become CIAM's worldwide design efforts, van Eyck suggested that non-Western architecture might have as much validity for the future as Western models. He also angrily rejected Walter Gropius's call at this event for standardization and teamwork with industry, as well as Gropius's attack there on "prima donna architects" like his old CIAM colleague Le Corbusier. Van Eyck and Bakema both shared an aversion to what they saw as an emerging postwar "system," one in which American consumerism was linked to its postwar military dominance and where the intangible social and artistic values of modern art were in danger.[5] At Aix this resistant attitude, which grew out of their quite different wartime experiences, found common cause with Georges Candilis's interests in engaging the problems of mass shelter in French North Africa. It was there that the Baku-born, Greek-educated architect had been active in the French Resistance in Algiers and then, after playing a central role alongside Le Corbusier on the design of the Unité d'Habitation in Marseille, had gone to Casablanca and Tangiers in 1949, to work with French planner Michel Ecochard in a CIAM group called ATBAT-Afrique. Candilis, Shadrach Woods, Vladimir Bodiansky (another Unité team-member), and others oversaw the design and construction of many housing and other projects throughout Morocco and Algeria until 1952, in an effort to address design for what Bodiansky termed "the greater number."[6] These prospective members of a new CIAM youth group made common cause at CIAM 9 with the newly arrived Peter and Alison Smithson (members of the British CIAM MARS group) and some other MARS youth members, including William Howell and John Voelcker.[7] The Smithsons were rising stars in Britain after winning the Hunstanton School competition in East Anglia, in 1949, with a severe Miesian design, but even before their epochal

CIAM grid presentation at Aix they had begun to experiment with large, proto-megastructural urban organizations that took the logic of the Unité and extended it to the design of campuses and urban districts. Although this direction had been anticipated in Le Corbusier's Algiers projects of the nineteen-thirties, the Smithsons' practice was also informed by their art world interests, which included the work of Jackson Pollock, then just emerging as the central figure in New York's Abstract Expressionist movement, European artists like Michel Tapié and Jean Dubuffet, and fellow members of the London Institute of Contemporary Art-based Independent Group such as Ed Paolozzi and Richard Hamilton.

The intent of the Smithsons' efforts to reorganize urban life along such radical lines was not simply formalistic. As the CIAM 9 grid presentation of their entry to the London Golden Lane mixed-use competition demonstrated, by using Nigel Henderson's photographs of Bethnal Green street children playing, their intent was to make "human association" a higher value in urbanism than the mere solution of the functional and technical requirements having to do with the provision of light, air circulation, green open spaces, and ease of transportation to work. They did not repudiate these CIAM values, and in fact the Smithsons later stressed their ties to CIAM and Le Corbusier, but they, quite parallel to the postwar CIAM of Sert (which they rejected), saw the housing environments produced by modern architecture as requiring additional places for community meeting. Unlike Sert, Ernesto Rogers, and Jaqueline Tyrwhitt's focus on "the heart of the city," the Smithsons were uninterested in civic plazas and the traditional places of public gathering celebrated at CIAM 8. Instead, they saw mobility and looser, more informal places of encounter as the qualities that modern architects should introduce into remade urban environments. They wanted to restore the prewar vitality of modern architecture by rejecting the Garden City and Scandinavian influenced British architecture of the immediate postwar years, which had been put on display at the Festival of Britain in 1951. Though they themselves were unable to realize their early nineteen-fifties competition designs, their topographical, socially-minded urbanistic ideas soon transformed British architecture, and housing projects like Park Hill in Sheffield (1956–61) by J. L. Womersley, Lynn & Smith, many new British

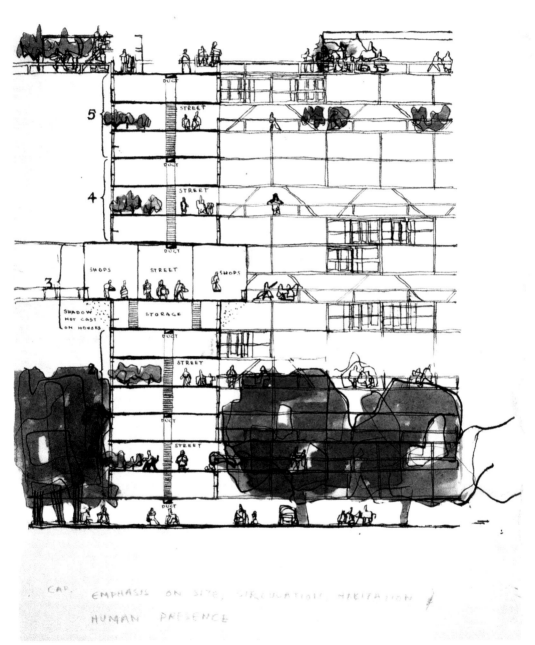

Alison and Peter Smithson, Panel from Golden Lane Housing competition, London, 1952. (Smithson Family Collection, London)

campus buildings of the nineteen-sixties, the entire London County Council (LCC) new town of Thamesmead (1967), and many other built projects demonstrate their worldwide influence.

By early 1954 Team 10 had issued its first manifesto in Doorn, the Netherlands, and the core figures of Team 10 were then asked to organize the tenth CIAM congress in Dubrovnik in 1956. They continued to meet as Team 10 in various western European settings until Bakema's death in 1981.[8] Their focus on urbanism and the way that architects might be able to shape urban patterns remained very much in line with CIAM's original intentions. Unlike CIAM, however, for Team 10 it was never entirely clear how their group organization was intended to function, or how it related to the larger client organizations involved in urban structuring. Instead of what to them seemed to be a reductive CIAM focus on functional zoning, basic standards, prototypes, and legislative procedures, Team 10 celebrated new urbanistic visions. In this way they extended the Corbusian model of the architect as a creative urban visionary into a shared vision that had parallels not only in art, but also in popular music.

Yet their wish to also make Team 10 a kind of think tank for new urban strategies in some ways contradicted this transformed genius-architect architectural ideal. To remain focused, Team 10 required a certain policing of dissenting views, a disturbing aspect of the group evident in the Smithsons' and Bakema's famous rejection of Ernesto Rogers's Torre Velasca in Milan, at the 1959 CIAM meeting in Otterlo, as "irresponsible."[9] For Team 10, Ernesto Rogers's error was to evoke the historic architecture of the city's Castello Sforzesco (1451–66) to bring modern architecture and technology in line with the traditional cultural forms of Italian urban life.[10] Instead of this Italian "neo-liberty" direction, the Smithsons, van Eyck, and Bakema all shared a wish to keep architecture real by providing new forms of urban organization for what they saw as the needs of the urban working classes, often using raw concrete surfaces, and not wasting design time or money on complex veneers and ornamental gestures. In doing so they thought the urban structuring of this new "brutalism" could better further social interaction and provide a public realm in the increasingly chaotic and confusing new postwar housing environments then being constructed around the world.

The various positive and negative aspects of the Team 10 approach can be clearly seen at one of their most important and intellectually vital meetings, held at Abbaye Royaumont in September 1962, in a former religious establishment that had been turned into a French government conference center. Alison Smithson, Bakema, Woods, and John Voelcker organized the event in Stockholm with the Swedish-English Team 10 member Ralph Erskine, and initially invited some forty architects, including Le Corbusier, Balkrishna Doshi, Kenzo Tange, Charles and Ray Eames, Jerzy Soltan, Lúcio Costa, Hans Scharoun, and Louis Kahn. None of those figures were able to attend, and ultimately about twenty guests were present. The exact list of participants may be impossible to reconstruct, as Alison Smithson deleted several of the presenters from the published proceedings.[11] The theme was to be the reciprocal relationship between building groups and infrastructure, a topic of great concern at the time as new housing projects and new expressway systems were transforming major industrial cities from London to Tokyo. Kenzo Tange's 1959 MIT studio project for Boston harbor, which he then developed into his Tokyo Bay plan of 1960, had proposed a transformation of the structural relationship between the dwelling unit and the city, and had enormous influence around the world at the time.[12] The Metabolist group he formed around him (which included Kiyonori Kikutake, Kisho Kurokawa, Fumihiko Maki, and others) also began to extend Team 10's urban-infrastructural ideas.[13]

Unlike the Smithsons, Tange had been receiving large urban commissions since the early nineteen-fifties, and he and some of the members of the Metabolists, like Maki, were closely linked to large Japanese construction and development companies, who eagerly sought their design advice in Japan's rapid postwar push to reconstruct wartime destruction and become the most developed country outside of Europe and North America. The Metabolist focus on demountable, prefabricated elements that could constantly be changed was theoretically carried even further in London, where in a parallel direction, Archigram (Peter Cook, Mike Webb, Dennis Crompton, Ron Herron, Warren Chalk, and others) soon emerged. Archigram's approach differed from that of the Smithsons not only in their Buckminster Fuller-inspired

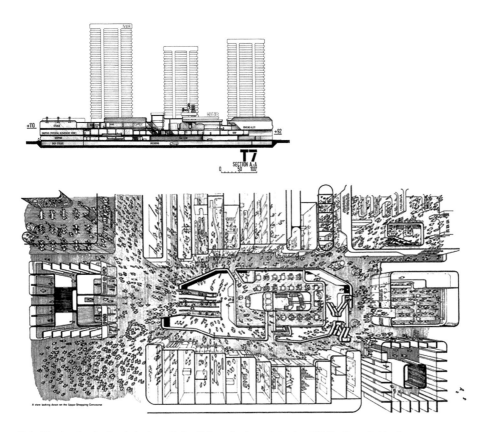

Taylor Woodrow Construction design team, Euston Station redevelopment, London, 1961 (Archigram Archives)

focus on lightweight and highly mobile elements, but also in their much greater willingness to embrace pop culture and the fast-expanding urban consumerist world of the early nineteen-sixties.

Many of the young members of Archigram were also working in British building and development agencies; Ron Herron had worked with the London County Council (LCC) Schools Division beginning in 1954, where he and Chalk designed the St. Pancras Starcross Secondary School for Girls (1957). They then joined forces with Crompton (until then a designer for MARS member Frederick Gibberd, architect of the Harlow New Town) to design the Team 10-like South Bank Arts Centre in 1960 for the LCC Special Works Division. This was immediately followed by work with Peter Cook at Taylor Woodrow Construction company, designing among other projects a vast redevelopment project for Euston, London with a design team that also included Robin Middleton and Brian Richards.[14]

In the carefully selected setting of Royaumont, the Smithsons sought to offer "models of method" for conceptualizing the design of infrastructure at the urban scale. Presentations included those of the Mozambique-based Amancio Guedes, James Stirling's presentation of his Leicester University Engineering Building (1960), Ralph Erskine's project for the Tibro housing area, in Brittgården, Sweden, and some southeast England metropolitan growth control proposals by John Voelcker.[15] These were followed by Peter Smithson's presentation of the London Roads Study (1959), an effort to consider how to best integrate new highway infrastructures into an existing urban fabric to create a stronger new sense of urban identity within particular districts, which he defined as urban "islands" bounded by the noise and energy of the main highways. Related issues were engaged in the Smithsons' presentation for "Citizen's Cambridge," where they proposed new parking garages be sited around the historic center to protect it from through traffic

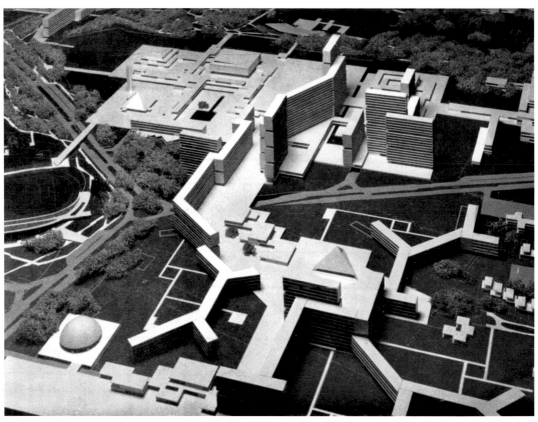

Candilis-Josic-Woods, Toulouse-le-Mirail new town, 1960-74. View of model (Avery Library Special Collections, Columbia University)

and overdevelopment, with a new shopping mall on the periphery. In its design diagram this project seems to evoke the work of Victor Gruen, particularly his "A Greater Ft. Worth Tomorrow" downtown pedestrianization proposal of 1956, but presented and discussed in an entirely different way. Instead of a focus on retaining the shopping and office vitality of a centralized downtown in the new era of express highway building, the Smithsons argued against any additional commercial development in the historic center, to keep rents low to allow small local businesses to flourish, and suggested that the new shopping mall be a place to put high rent uses, notably supermarkets.[16]

Far more engaged with actual large building bureaucracies at this time were Candilis-Josic-Woods, major figures in the massive construction of peripheral new towns and social housing developments in France in the nineteen-fifties.[17] Paralleling the Smithsons' interest in the effects of mobility and dense commercial development, it was at Royaumont that Shadrach Woods presented the

firm's competition entry for the urbanization of the Asua Valley near Bilbao, Spain. This was a scheme similar to their two French new town projects designed for the French government in 1961, Caen-Hérouville and Toulouse-le-Mirail, the latter also presented at Royaumont.[18] The Asua Valley project called for linking around fifty large, ten-story residential slab buildings into a new urban organization, joined by lowrise linear pedestrian "stems" with public uses. As at their built Toulouse project, their goal was to provide a new form of continuous pedestrian-oriented urban development to counter the isolated towers set in open space of postwar mass housing, which for Team 10 defined the essence of CIAM urbanism. Woods believed that "the structure of cities lies not in their geometries but in the activities within them," which are "expressed or materialized by buildings and spaces, by ways and places, by the articulation of the public and private domains."[19] In this articulation, he noted that a key issue was the "reconciliation of speeds" between cars and pedestrians, and his firm designed

Piet Blom, Noah's Ark urbanization project for the Amsterdam region, 1959. Model of one neighborhood (Abel Blom).

such that private car journeys were "point to point," ending in cul-de-sacs linked to parking structures within the towers, while pedestrian movement in the stem elements was to be more direct and open-ended. Woods saw these projects less as final master plans than as an expression of a "way of planning."[20]

Among the other Team 10 and invited presentations at Royaumont, which included megastructural projects by Jacob Bakema, Giancarlo de Carlo, José Coderch, and Stefan Wewerka, the Metabolist Kisho Kurokawa's presentation of his idea of a capsule tower, later built as the Nakagin Capsule Tower in Tokyo,[21] a contentious debate stands out. This involved a dispute over the nature of urbanism itself, between core Team 10 members Aldo van Eyck and the Smithsons. Van Eyck presented two student projects from his teaching at the Amsterdam Academy of Art, one of which, by Piet Blom and called "Noah's Ark," was a gigantic urban design scheme for housing a million people by linking sixty villages around Amsterdam into a "interurban entity" of seventy villages

of ten to fifteen thousand people. Each sixty hectare village was organized into interlocking built clusters that provided for a range of urban functions, all tied together by a four-level road network. By making the traffic infrastructure a basic part of the project, Blom proposed the total integration of infrastructure and building groups within it.[22]

Royaumont guests Guillermo Jullian de la Fuente (Le Corbusier's design associate at this time), Kurokawa, Wewerka, and Guedes all admired the scheme, but the Smithsons and Voelcker were highly critical. In his presentation van Eyck had referred to Leon Battista Alberti's well-known analogy that the city should be like a large house, with each part characterized by both enclosure and openness. These ideas were related to van Eyck's efforts to develop a "configurative discipline" of urbanism, where he took issue with the then widely accepted idea that architects should build for the anonymous ideal client of government housing corporations. Instead, architects should provide "urban interiors . . . built coun-

Van den Broek and Bakema, Bochum University competition, 1962 (Bakema and Opbouw collection, Netherlands Architecture Institute, Rotterdam)

terforms" to reinforce identity, such as those already found in vernacular villages and towns from around the world like those of the Dogon of Mali or the Native American Zunis of New Mexico. Van Eyck saw the Blom project as an excellent demonstration of these ideas, a city as "a hierarchy of superimposed configurative systems multilaterally conceived."[23]

The Smithsons vehemently objected to the project's repetitiveness, and Alison saw it as a "completely Fascist" attempt to control all aspects of future urban growth, thus ending van Eyck's efforts to develop his new urbanistic discipline within the framework of Team 10. Le Corbusier and Jullian de la Fuente on the other hand found it to be their major inspiration in the unbuilt Venice Hospital project (1963).[24]

In the discussion of Blom's project, Van Eyck had added to the city/house metaphor of the city by invoking the idea that it should have a tree/leaf structure, where the detailed organization of the leaf is then mirrored at a larger scale in the tree itself, or as he put in his famous leaf-tree diagram, "tree is leaf and leaf is tree—house is

city and city is house."[25] In response Christopher Alexander, the Vienna-born, Cambridge educated recent Harvard PhD then working in rural development in India, pointed out that the structure of a leaf is not that of a tree. At Royaumont he had described how his efforts to quantify the various functional needs required in the design of an Indian rural village had produced an early computer-based method to organize patterns of functional needs in a series of linked categories, which he would soon publish after Royaumont as Notes on the Synthesis of Form (1964), and then develop into his concept of a pattern language. By using this mathematically generated (though not statistically based) method, Alexander argued against van Eyck that "a city is not a tree," in that a city does not have a hierarchical tree-like structure, but can instead be represented by a semi-lattice diagram of overlapping functional and cultural linkages.[26]

The Royaumont meeting perhaps marked the high point of Team 10's efforts to continue CIAM-like deliberations on the future of architects' relation to urbanism, but the proceedings show that no general agreement was pos-

sible there. Van Eyck would go on to be a major influence on Dutch Structuralism and the work of figures like Hermann Hertzberger, but this direction would have little in common with the Smithsons' and Candilis-Josic-Woods's ultimately doomed efforts to restructure urban industrial societies in vast new megastructures. Yet the meeting and Team 10 and its successor groups like the Metabolists and Archigram did suggest some new models that lay between Hitchcock's architecture of bureaucracy and architecture of genius. In all three groups, many of the members were then actively proposing, and in some cases implementing, new models of collaborative design with industry to produce new urban environments.

In this it was perhaps only possible for the designers to avoid the deadening effects of bureaucratic standardization by carrying forward the aura of celebrity architects, without necessarily being able to reconcile the tensions in the field that Hitchcock had identified, and which remain unresolved to the present day.

1   Henry-Russell Hitchcock, "The Architecture of Bureaucracy and the Architecture of Genius." *Architectural Review* 101 (January 1947), pp. 1–3.

2   On Oak Ridge, see Nicholas Adams, *Skidmore, Owings & Merrill: SOM since 1936* (Milan, 2006), p. 24.

3   Hitchcock 1947 (see note 1), pp. 4–6.

4   Some other young CIAM members considered ended up not being part of Team 10, including the British protégé of Jaqueline Tyrwhitt, William Howell; James Stirling; the Norwegian architect and historian Christian Norberg-Schultz; and Sigfried Giedion's son-in-law, Paffard Keatinge Clay.

5   Cornelis Wagenaar, "Jaap Bakema and the Fight for Freedom," in Sarah Williams Goldhagen and Réjean Legault, eds. *Anxious Modernisms* (Montreal and Cambridge, MA, 2000), pp. 266, 270–72; Frances Strauven, *Aldo van Eyck: The Shape of Relativity* (Amsterdam, 1998), pp. 223–30.

6   On the context of ATBAT-Afrique, see Jean-Louis Cohen and Monique Eleb, *Casablanca: Colonial Myths and Architectural Ventures* (New York, 1992), pp. 301–63. For a brief account of the formation of what became Team 10 at the postwar CIAMs, see Strauven, 238–79. One of the first efforts to provide a canonical account of the group was "Team 10 + 20," *L'architecture d'aujourd'hui* 177 (January/February 1975), which included Kenneth Frampton's important essay, "The Vicissitudes of Ideology," pp. 62–66.

7   According to Alison Smithson, she and Peter were on CIAM 9 Commission 6 on the Charter of Habitat with William and Gillian Howell, Shad Woods, Aldo van Eyck, and Sandy van Ginkel (Alison Smithson, Team 10 Meetings 1953–1984 [New York, 1991], p. 19). The unpublished CIAM 9 documents list the Smithsons along with some thirty other CIAM members on Commission 6, "social questions." This committee was co-chaired by

three CIAM members, Pierre-André Emery, Georges Candilis, and either the Swedish historian and architect Gregor Paulsson, or the Swiss CIAM member Alfred Roth, and listed among the Commission 6 members Balkrishna Doshi, Fernando Tavora, Roland Simounet, William Howell, and Ernst May, but not Woods, van Eyck, or van Ginkel, who were on other Commissions at this meeting (CIAM 9: Aix-en-Provence, 19–26 Juillet 1953: Rapport des commissions, ETHZ CIAM archive, CIAM-42-JT-X).

8    Max Risselada and Dirk van den Heuvel, *Team 10: In Search of a Utopia of the Present, 1953–81* (Rotterdam, 2004).

9    Oscar Newman, ed., *CIAM '59 in Otterlo* (Stuttgart, 1961), p. 95.

10    The wider Italian context of this debate at Otterlo is discussed in Sara Protasoni, "The Italian Group and the Modern Tradition," *Rassegna* 52/1 (December 1992), pp. 28–32.

11    According to Risselada and van den Heuvel (see note 8, pp. 99–101), the architects who attended who were not listed were Le Corbusier's associate, Guillermo Jullian de la Fuente, Fernando Távora, Luis Miquel, André Schimmerling, Colin St. John Wilson, and James Stirling. Oscar Hansen is also listed as attending in Strauven 1998 (see note 5), p. 397.

12    See Rem Koolhaas and Hans Ulrich Obrist, *Project Japan: Metabolism Talks* (Cologne, 2011).

13    Team 10 invited Maki to their Bagnols-sur Céze meeting in 1960 to present his Group Form ideas, which differed from those of the other Metabolists in being more about how discrete building elements can be assembled to produce a collective image where the individual elements can change over time, much as in traditional vernacular villages. See Fumihiko Maki, *Nurturing Dreams: Collected Essays on Architecture and the City* (Cambridge, MA, 2008), pp. 31–32.

14    Simon Sadler, *Archigram: Architecture without Architecture* (Cambridge, MA, 2005), pp. 10–33, 45–46; *Architectural Design* (November 1975), pp. 682–83. Brian Richards also attended the Royaumont meeting with Christopher Dean and presented their own unbuilt Euston station megastructure project there, "Team 10 at Royaumont," *Architectural Design* (November 1975), p. 682.

15    The Guedes, Erskine, and Voelcker projects are discussed in "Team 10 at Royaumont," (see note 14), pp. 666–68; 670–71; 672–73.

16    "Peter Smithson: Team 10 at Royaumont," in ibid., pp. 674–75. These proceedings were republished with slightly different illustrations in Smithson 1991 (see note 7), pp. 37–97.

17    See Tom Avermaete, *Another Modern: The Post-war Architecture and Urbanism of Candilis-Josic-Woods* (Rotterdam, 2005).

18    "Team 10 at Royaumont" (see note 14), pp. 687–89. These projects are illustrated in detail in Shadrach Woods, *Candilis-Josic-Woods: Building for People* (New York, 1968), pp. 174–99.

19    "Team 10 at Royaumont" (see note 14), p. 174.

20    Ibid., pp. 684–86.

21    Ibid., p. 677.

22    Strauven 1998 (see note 5), pp. 372–75. Alison Smithson did not include any illustrations of Blom's project in her many Team 10 related publications, thus ensuring its relative obscurity even today.

23    Aldo van Eyck, Forum 3, 92; quoted and discussed in Strauven 1998 (see note 5), pp. 367–79.

24    This debate and its implications for van Eyck's efforts to create a "configurative discipline" of urbanism is described in detail in Strauven 1998 (see note 5), pp. 397–406.

25    "Team 10 at Royaumont"; reprinted in Smithson 1991 (see note 7), pp. 76–79.

26    Christopher Alexander, "A City is Not a Tree," *Architectural Forum* (April 1965), pp. 58–62, and *Architectural Forum* (May 1965), pp. 58–61. Part 2 is republished with notes in Joan Ockman, ed. *Architecture Culture 1943–1968* (New York, 1993), pp. 379–88.

Womb Chair Prototype, 1946 (photo: Harvey Croze)

# Innovate/Test/Apply:
## Collaborating with Industry at Eero Saarinen Associates

## Eeva-Liisa Pelkonen

"From the miraculous potentials of engineering and science will come new possibilities, new materials and new problems. These will have to be absorbed."
—Eero Saarinen, 1957

The American contribution to modern architecture in the course of twentieth century was based on two opposite models of practice: the studio-style atelier model, organized around towering individuals such as Louis Sullivan and Frank Lloyd Wright, and the rise of the collaborative practice during the postwar era. The story of Skidmore, Owings and Merrill (SOM) is now well known; three individuals, none of whom might have had the design talents to compete on their own, forming a partnership in the late nineteen-thirties, which grew to become the largest architectural firm in the world. The phenomenal success of SOM relied from the very start on the realization that the making of architecture requires diverse skills and benefits from collective intelligence.[1]

The story of the firm Eero Saarinen and Associates (1950–65) forms a bridge between these two models of practice. Unlike SOM, ESA was founded and centered on the head designer, but soon grew into a partnership. Tellingly, John Dinkeloo, who became a partner heading the practice's research and development arm and overseeing the execution of projects, joined the office in 1950 after working at the Chicago office of SOM. Joe Lacey became the business partner, which underscores the fact that while realizing that architecture was indeed a business, Saarinen rather needed somebody else do that part of the practice. As with SOM, all ESA partners thus had diverse talents.

Therefore, while the name of the ESA office referred to only one man, Saarinen never worked alone, but was able to capitalize on the talents of his partners as well as the energies of the many brilliantly talented people who shared his daring spirit. Office photographs often show Saarinen among a group of young employees working on the large-scale models used to solve complicated formal and structural problems.

Eero Saarinen and Associates' contribution to postwar architecture was similarly two-fold: to be sure, the office built many iconic buildings that bear Saarinen's idiosyncratic formal stamp, but one must be reminded that these buildings were also an outcome of teamwork and their success relied on the development of new building materials and technologies, which in turn relied on an intense collaboration with the building industry. Importantly, while SOM was based in New York, Saarinen's office was located in Bloomfield Hills, Michigan, just outside Detroit, the center of America's (indeed, the world's) automobile industry. Timing also mattered: Saarinen established his office in 1950, at the beginning of a decade marked by American economic growth, technological prowess, and political might. The pace of technological innovation and growth was enormous in the immediate aftermath of the war; old industries grew while new ones were born, often as by-products of wartime technologies. Saarinen believed strongly that architecture should keep up with these developments.

The location of the office helped in this regard, since the massive presence of the automobile factories had provided the Detroit area with a wealth of subcontractors supplying specialty production tooling, services, and parts. One could compare the Detroit of the nineteen-fifties to contemporary Silicon Valley: a hotbed of innovation and experimentation. As Kevin Roche, an Irish-born architect who joined the office in 1950 recalls: "You could get anything made in Detroit [at that time]."

Saarinen also benefited from the huge postwar construction boom. The GI Bill called for the expansion of higher education facilities, returning veterans required the construction of new housing; and expanding American industries demanded the construction of new office and manufacturing sites. Saarinen worked productively in all these areas. Nowhere else in the world were the scale of the projects and the ambitions as great as in the United States during the nineteen-fifties. At that time, the total output of building totaled some $44.1 billion dollars, having grown fourfold between 1946 and 1956.[2]

Saarinen's clients included some of the biggest and most powerful companies in the country: General Motors, then the largest company in the United States and the largest employer in the world; IBM, a pioneer in the area of emerging information technologies; and Bell Labs, the leading inventor of communication technology, from early transistors to semiconductors.[3] Significantly, all of these companies considered architecture and design an important part of their business model. The sheer size of these corporate architectural commissions and their budgets made ambitious product development feasible.

With such youth, vigor, economic prosperity, and corporate support during its fifteen-year existence, Eero Saarinen Associates can be credited for pioneering entire ranges of new products and standards, many of which are now widely accepted throughout the architecture and building industry.

In this essay I explore Saarinen's collaboration with various industries, and the ESA experimental approach to research and development, which led to many breakthrough innovations in curtain wall technology, such as the initial architectural application of Cor-Ten steel, and later the invention and employment of mirrored glass.[4] I will also discuss his collaborations with individuals, which included at different times his friend Charles Eames, his design associate Kevin Roche, and his partner John Dinkeloo. After Saarinen's untimely death in 1961, the latter two led the effort to complete the remaining Saarinen oeuvre; their firm Kevin Roche John Dinkeloo and Associates (KRJDA) was established in 1965 after the Saarinen mission was complete. In an open-ended conclusion, I will evaluate Saarinen's legacy as a technical innovator and speculate upon the equivalent opportunities in contemporary practice at the time when the architectural world tends to become increasingly dominated by large corporate firms.

## Material Applications and Transfers

To be sure, Saarinen stayed true to his words quoted above that in order to stay relevant he believed that architects had to "absorb" the trends and pace of technology. Saarinen often used a wide range of newly patented and newly available material products; this consistent approach testifies to his ambition and ability to keep up with the cutting edge of technological development. One of the architect's greatest legacies remains the development of new building materials and technical solutions based on technology transfers from other industries. These often daring innovations and applications demanded close collaboration with various manufacturers, with subsequent material testing, and extensive prototyping. In many cases, these experiments set new industry standards. As a testimony to Saarinen's professionalism, combined with his far-sightedness, many of these products—mirrored glass being one—are still in wide use.

The first area of material experimentations occurred with a series of chair designs beginning in 1940 and continued for a decade. The first chair emerged as the winning entry of the 1940 Organic Design in Home Furnishing competition organized by The Museum of Modern Art. Together with Charles Eames, a friend at Cranbrook,[5] Saarinen submitted an entry which consisted of a series of upholstered molded plywood living room chairs. A design relying on plywood bent in two directions would not have been possible had Saarinen not been aware of the recent developments in curved plywood technology. Don Albison, who worked on the project, recalls: "In Germany, in 1914 and 1915, they were molding three-dimensional curved plywood fuselages for Albatross fighters.... By 1940 there was a lot of three-dimensional formed plywood out there. Eero discovered that the patent for three-dimensional formed plywood belonged to a man named Haskell in Grand Rapids, Michigan."[6] According to Albison, Eames and Saarinen visited the Haskelite Corporation and found the production capabilities they needed for the chairs. Only some one hundred chairs were produced by this method, however, as World War II halted the availability of both plywood (used for the seating form) and aluminum, which was used for the chair's legs. Nevertheless, the experimentation with parallel industrial developments in materials and fabrication

General Motors Technical Center, mock-up of the illuminated ceiling, 1949

techniques was a notable instance in which Saarinen cross-fertilized building and design with development achieved in a different industry, in this case airplane manufacturing.

With the Womb chair, designed and developed in 1948, Saarinen moved beyond plywood to employ reinforced polyester resin, a material which had been developed during World War II for the hulls of US Navy boats. The material allowed the chair to be light and to be constructed as a single piece. The prototypes were commissioned from a Trenton, New Jersey, boat company, Winner Manufacturing, which had been involved in the war effort. The collaboration with Winner led to the development of "resin-bonded fiber shells, where fiber reinforcing material was impregnated with a low-pressure bonding resin, and placed in a mold that utilized a vacuum bag for forming the shell."[7] The fiber at that time was sisal, while glass fiber was used for the later versions of the chair. Winner also helped produce the one-legged Pedestal chair in 1957, which then went into production the following year.

General Motors Technical Center, curtain wall mock-up, 1949 (General Motors)

Saarinen's first major commission, The General Motors Technical Center, a project encompassing a twenty-five-building campus in Warren, Michigan (1948–56), became a large-scale laboratory for product development and material experimentation, not least because of the size of the project. General Motors was at that time America's largest corporation and the $100 million dollar building complex was the world's most expensive building project (today this cost would equal close to one billion dollars).

General Motors Technical Center, Installation of neoprene gaskets (photo: Lionel Freedman, General Motors)

General Motors Technical Center, Finished curtain wall with neoprene caskets (photo: GM Photographic)

Many pioneering technological innovations and new material products were developed for the General Motors project, in collaboration with the corporation and with local industries. The two-inch thick panels for the curtain wall were developed in collaboration with a local porcelain-enamel firm. The light-diffusing illuminated ceiling with integrated lighting fixtures and sprinkler systems required collaborations with Rohm & Haas, a local manufacturer of the Plexiglas acrylic sheet, as well as Cadillac Plastics, manufacturer of the light diffusers, and the Wakefield Company, which manufactured the lighting units.[8] In order to produce the colored glazed bricks for the buildings, General Motors actually purchased a brick burning facility and even subsequently marketed the bricks as a product, a sign that GM understood the building industry as a viable area of expansion to their business. The automobile manufacturer even considered expanding into the housing market by commissioning Saarinen to design a prototypical house in 1955—with an integrated carport, of course!

The metal panel curtain wall for General Motors was the subject of the most research, development, and testing.

The first version had already been imagined in 1946 at the office of Saarinen, Swanson, Swanson, led by Eero Saarinen's father Eliel, who had received the original GM commission and who had designed the first (unbuilt) version that year. The final curtain wall panel design was just two inches thick, consisting of gray steel panels sandwiching a honeycomb core filled with perlite, a granular insulation material. The porcelain enamel panels soon became the industry standard, with Saarinen's office leading the way to new, ever thinner versions, including the five-sixteenth-inch panels employed in IBM's Manufacturing and Training Facility in Rochester, Minnesota (1956–58). Although the first versions of the curtain wall for the General Motors Technical Center were sealed with caulk, Saarinen and his team learned again from the automotive industry and shifted to the use of neoprene, "zipper" gaskets, which had been quickly adopted by automobile manufacturers only after neoprene had become widely available for commercial use after the war.[9]

Taking another note from the automotive industry, Saarinen introduced the use of full-scale mock-ups into building design during the General Motors project to test

Deere and Company Administrative Center, façade mock-up, 1960. (Photo: R K Sunderbruch).

his daring curtain wall paneling system. The first such model was constructed in 1949, a somewhat crude structure with wood sides that tested simultaneously the proportions of panels and the technical feasibility of the product. The full-scale mock-up allowed different parties to work simultaneously on a design problem, to test solutions, and to communicate ideas during the design and construction process. Saarinen studied how the automobile industry used full-scale mock-ups, evolving car designs in cycles of research and input, and testing and corrections.[10] Charles Eames saw a parallel between Saarinen's "operations research"-based design approach and the systems analysis approach to problem solving developed during World War II and then appropriated by American industry during the postwar years. He later recalled:

> Industrial research vocabulary and procedures accorded in many ways with Eero's fondness for testing by models, both abstract and concrete; innovative building elements were tested at full scale, in real conditions, over time. Energy and experience from each stage of construction were fed back to the successive ones, to upgrade the details and materials. Surface finishes were changed and changed again; aluminum glazing strips gave way to precisely detailed neoprene gaskets, as the same new techniques were incorporated in GM's assembly lines.[11]

Importantly, design and execution was never conceived as a one-way street but involved continuous feedback and readjustments, which required architects to develop communication skills and tools. Eames concludes his assessment of Saarinen's design approach at General Motors at follows: "By the time the [GM] center was completed, Eero had become a master of the feedback principle; he had found confirmation of his natural commitment to systems, but he did not narrow it to technical applications. He retained from then on the capacity to sit down and really communicate with engineers and businessmen."[12]

Saarinen's sudden death in 1961 placed Kevin Roche and John Dinkeloo into leading roles for the practice; Roche took charge of design direction and Dinkeloo assumed responsibility for the execution of projects. Their immedi-

# THE BIGGEST MIRROR EVER

ARCHITECTURAL FORUM_April, 1967

Bell Telephone Corporation Laboratories featured in *Architectural Forum,* April, 1967

ate challenges were to complete the works started by and commissioned to Saarinen, a set of projects concluded in 1965 with the completion of the St. Louis Gateway Arch. That same year, the two renamed their office Kevin Roche John Dinkeloo and Associates.

## Developing New Building Materials

Eero Saarinen's ability to create an atmosphere of innovation and creativity inside the practice was cherished by Roche and Dinkeloo, who, together with their boss, formed an ideal team for generating numerous ideas for new materials and products. The ESA design team rarely settled for applying existing products, but often had to (or were compelled to) develop and launch new products. Two notable emblematic examples are the Cor-Ten steel specified for the John Deere and Sons Headquarters in Moline, Illinois (1957–63), and the mirrored glass panels for the curtain wall for the Bell Headquarters in Holmdel,

New Jersey (1957–62), now both standard products. Both projects and products demonstrate how a single architectural project can pioneer an entirely new product; such daring innovations took immense collaborative design, research and production effort. Saarinen's specification of Cor-Ten steel, a product developed in the nineteen-thirties primarily for the use of coal train tracks for the John Deere and Company Administrative Center is such a story of architectural design research and intensive material testing. The identification and subsequent architectural development of Cor-Ten steel illustrates the ESA team's open-minded, systems- and research-based approach to solutions. After deciding that the Deere headquarters would be an exposed structural steel frame building, the ESA team began to explore solutions to protect the steel. At the onset of the Deere commission, Cor-Ten steel had only recently attained sufficient corrosion protection guarantees to make it suit-

Dulles International Airport, mobile lounge model, c.1958

able for wider industrial applications. Roche and Din-keloo's awareness of this development is but one exam-ple among many of their ability to track technological improvements and breakthroughs in other industries. Dinkeloo recalls: "In the search we came across an inter-esting corrosion chart put out by U.S. Steel, which com-pares corrosion between ordinary structural steel and high-strength, low-alloy steel. All three materials start out with a fairly rapid rate of corrosion, but then high-strength steel tapers off."[13] Parallel to the emphasis on materials research, the ESA office also emphasized the use of full-scale construction systems mock-ups in the design pro-cess. A two-story-high mock-up was used not only to test the architectural application of a material, but to sell the idea to the client as well. In the case of the John Deere project and Cor-Ten, the mock-up was a two-story high segment of the actual building; the testing was doubly complex due to the very nature of the material, as yet untried for architectural purposes. The challenge in this phase was to assess and optimize the level of corrosion on the Cor-Ten, subject to time and weather conditions from the start. Questions were asked throughout the pro-cess: "How would horizontal and vertical surfaces vary in wetting? How would wetting affect rivet and bolt fasten-ing?"[14] In addition, the question of what the material would look like after exposure over various time periods was an important factor; the ESA design team eventually settled for a deeply colored brown. In this case, the data was fed back to US Steel, the product's manufacturer and patent holder, to further develop their product for architectural use. The project, completed in 1963, helped to optimize and promote Cor-Ten steel for wider architec-tural use and the product has become a significant mate-rial in contemporary architecture over the last forty years.

A second instructive case of ESA's material experimen-tation and product development is the development of mirrored glass for the Bell Laboratories in Holmdel, New Jersey (1957–62). As with Cor-Ten steel, the material's origins lie in the combination of practicality, sheer new-ness, and symbolic allure of the material—and again, from an openness to the idea of using a material from an industry completely unrelated to architecture and the building industry. Bell's mirror-glass is also a story of how innovation can derive as much through happenstance and even wild speculation, in lines of thought that steer away from direct practical emphasis. For as Roche recalls, the idea germinated in an advertisement for sun-glasses:

> *Life* magazine had a front-page photograph of a man with reflecting sunglasses on, and it occurred to me: if you can put reflecting sun-glasses on, why can't you do that to a building and avoid the sun glare and the sun heat. So, John got interested in that idea. John ran with the reflecting glass idea and went to a small firm called Detroit Glass. One of the interesting things about Detroit postwar was that there were all kinds of small industries that had been set up around the automobile industry and the war effort. You could actually achieve almost any-thing because you had all of these entrepreneur-ial types with backyard firms who were very gung-ho and eager to do things. So, Detroit Glass—and I don't remember the man's name—really ran with the idea.

Finding manufacturers proved to be tricky at times. Roche continues his story:

> [In order to get it into large-scale production] Eero and John and I went to Libbey Owens Ford, which was in Toledo, and we secured a meeting with the Chairman of the Board. We took along a piece of this reflecting glass and we went into a pitch about this is the glass of the future, and all that. They were totally not interested—abso-lutely not. They almost threw us out. They had absolutely no interest whatsoever. Pittsburgh Glass did pick it up subsequently and it became a very large item in the evolution of glass and

energy and all of those things. But it also of course raised the hackles of many of those people who didn't like the idea of mirrored buildings.[15]

The episode demonstrates how a very few creative and daring individuals, working with small companies, can outsmart a large corporation in spotting trends. Yet neither Dinkeloo and Roche, nor the man at Detroit Glass, could have imagined in their wildest dreams the viral dissemination of the product into the built environment: an architecturally-scaled "box" with a mirrored glass skin is now a ubiquitous sight around the globe. As the years passed, Dinkeloo's ambitions for innovations of this kind grew in regards to the potentials of the building industry: rather than simply coming up with new products, he wanted to transform the building industry to be more capable of innovation. For Dinkeloo, architecture did not progress through new forms, but through careful research and development based on the coordinated effort of architects, engineers, and manufacturers. In a 1967 lecture at the American Institute of Architects annual meeting in New York City, he dreamed of a future "where we would no longer have thousands of manufacturers, subcontractors, and general contractors, but probably a few very large organizations, such as the automotive industry, and it would disrupt the entire manufacturing and building set up completely." To achieve this end, Dinkeloo proposed a myriad of models, such as think thanks and research consortiums involving architects, engineers and manufacturers, to radically expand conventional models of architectural collaboration and practice: "The architect has to find ways of creating teams of engineers, manufacturers, or research potential on a large scale that includes all facets of the industry either by having the possibility of a profit motivation or by large government grants. If [the building industry] is to really succeed, it has to be the size of our government's aerospace program...."[16] For Dinkeloo, the shift in scale changed the paradigm: the architect was no longer a master builder, but one of many actors in this new giant research and development apparatus.

Dinkeloo's insights and proposals resound those of Jack Burnham, the leading protagonist of systems theory in art in the nineteen-sixties, who called for a general shift from "an object-orientated culture to a systems-orien-

tated" culture. Dinkeloo's thoughts reflect a growing frustration that the building industry was hopelessly lagging behind other industries in terms of innovation and efficiency. Having earlier helped to pioneer many small-scale material products, he now envisioned a large-scale transformation in industry, believing that only the introduction of a different economy of scale—a large-scale project like General Motors or a large-scale reformulation of an entire industry or profession—allowed the necessary level of product development and testing. Yet, herein is the paradox: innovation needs both an economy of scale, that is, architectural projects that are large enough to facilitate complicated and extensive testing, yet by and large, despite its size and reach, the large building industry has proven to be one of the least innovative industries, partly due to code restrictions and complicated materials approval processes. Small is still beautiful.

**Conclusion**

There are certainly lessons to be learned from ESA's legacy. Importantly, the most lasting innovations pioneered by Saarinen's office pertain to materials, rather than typologies. The mobile lounge developed for Dulles International Airport in Chantilly, Virginia, for example, never became an industry standard, while many of Saarinen's material innovations are still around.

The most important lesson Saarinen's practice might provide to today's young practitioners is that innovation is always a product of both individual imagination and daring and a climate of collaboration between architects and industry. Furthermore, for Saarinen technological innovation always went always hand in hand with a desire to embody formal and aesthetic ideas and vice versa: formal vision was backed by the appropriate technological tools.

The main lesson of Saarinen's office might well be that the only way to compete with much larger entities, such as SOM, relies on the combination of strong design and technological innovation. Furthermore, even today, collaboration with small workshops and manufacturers, who might be more willing to take more risks than large, often more rigid corporate builders, might yield best results. The same goes to the size of the architectural office: staying relatively small as a practice might enable archi-

tecture firms to stay more nimble and more innovative.
The fundamentals for replicating Saarinen's success as
a formal and technological innovator are there. Indeed,
we are living in an exciting time, both in terms of technological innovation and a relatively robust building industry worldwide. As with Saarinen's practice half a century
ago, new firms are tapping into new technologies in a
nimble manner; firms such as SHoP are leading the way.
New digital tools fuel continued formal innovation but
they also allow new forms of collaboration across the
globe. However, unlike the conditions that encouraged
Saarinen, the contemporary moment still lacks what
might be understood as "the missing links" of governmental and corporate support: one has yet to see what
types of innovative architecture, if any, and innovative
material and building technologies, today's enlightened
governments and today's leading industrial centers,
such as Silicon Valley, might sponsor.

1  My discussion of SOM is informed by Nicholas Adams's excellent
*Skidmore, Owings & Merrill: SOM Since 1936* (Milan, 2006).

2  Ian McCallum, Foreword to "Machine-Made America," *Architectural
Review* (May 1957), p. 296.

3  Bell Labs was acquired by Alcatel-Lucent in the nineteen-nineties. Kevin
Roche John Dinkeloo and Associates has completed two major buildings for
Lucent since then.

4  My article owes to and builds on the research conducted by numerous
scholars who were part of the curatorial research team for the exhibition and
book *Eero Saarinen: Shaping the Future*, which I helped lead. For more
information on the technological aspects of Saarinen's work see articles by
Rosamond Fletches, Brian Lutz, and Reinhold Martin in the catalog *Eero
Saarinen: Shaping the Future*, Eeva-Liisa Pelkonen and Donald Albrecht,
eds. (New Haven, 2006).

5  Saarinen and Eames met at Cranbrook, where Saarinen returned after
completing his architectural studies at Yale. Working briefly as a studio
instructor. The two became fast friends and life-long collaborators. For
details regarding Saarinen's life and career see "Chronology" in Pelkonen,
Albrecht 2006 (see note 4) .

6  Don Albison in Museum of Modern Art, Project in Home Furnishings
report, June 24, 1940. Quoted by Brian Lutz in "Furniture, Form and Innovation," in Pelkonen, Albrecht 2006 (see note 4), p. 248.

7  Lutz, ibid.

8  See "Investment in Tomorrow" in *Rohn & Haas Reporter* (May–June,
1956), which discusses the illuminated ceiling in great detail.

9  http://www2.dupont.com/Phoenix_Heritage/en_US/1931_c_detail.html.
Accessed 4/23/2012.

10  My discussion of the GM Tech center is informed by Rosamond
Fletcher's well-researched essay "The General Motors Technical Center; a
Collaborative Enterprise" in Pelkonen, Albrecht 2006 (see note 4), which
was part of her M.E.D. thesis at Yale, "Negotiating the Interface: Communi-
cation and Collaboration in Building Technology, from Graphic Manuals to
Software" (Yale University, 2005).

11  Charles Eames, "General Motors Revisited," *Architectural Forum* (June
1971), p. 25

12  Ibid., p. 26.

13  John Dinkeloo, "The Steel with Weather Naturally," *Architectural
Record* (August 1962), p. 148.

14 Ibid., p. 150.

15  See "Kevin Roche in His Own Words, " in Eeva-Liisa Pelkonen, *Kevin
Roche: Architecture as Environment* (New Haven, 2011), p. 264.

16  John Dinkeloo, Lecture given at the AIA convention in New York City,
July 1967. Unpublished manuscript, John Dinkeloo Papers, Yale University
Manuscripts and Archives, p. 5. Uncatalogued.

Make-a-thon: an IDEO prototype event experimenting with design-driven collaboration

# Teamwork in Practice
## Peter MacKeith

*"Teamwork in Practice," is a discussion led by Peter MacKeith, between principal designers Michael Bierut of Pentagram and Sandy Speicher of IDEO focusing on their respective firms' collaborative approaches and inter-disciplinary design practices. It is, in fact, itself an exercise in collaboration across the design culture, with the ambition to draw upon the wisdom of those engaged in modes of design practice different from that of SOM, either in scale of practice, or in design character all together. Based on the belief that architecture can learn more for its sustenance from other creative fields, whether the visual arts, the literary arts, or the design arts, these discussions are the first in a set of comparative case studies of teamwork in design and in the related arts—film and animation production, furniture and industrial design, communications design, and strategic design.*

*Michael Bierut is a partner in the New York office of the international consultancy Pentagram, a founder of the website DesignObserver.com, and a senior critic in graphic design at Yale University's School of Art. Sandy Speicher leads IDEO's Design for Learning domain, which brings human-centered thinking to systemic challenges in education. While much of her work has focused on education, Sandy has a broad range of experience leading and contributing to programs in the areas of hospitality, telecommunications, healthcare, and social innovation.*

*Directed discussions with Bierut and Speicher produced engaging perceptions of the challenges and value of collaborative work, ranging from the perceptions of "signature-less" practice to the development of firm-wide cultures of teamwork. Bierut observes a productive "tension between independence and collectivism" in Pentagram's office structure and work, and Speicher asserts the "humility, support of creativity, and a belief in collective wisdom deeply embedded in IDEO's culture"; both practices thrive without "a name on the door" by virtue of these methods and approaches.*

**PM:** Pentagram and IDEO as design practices each possess both a strong, simple signifier as title—a firm name which does not identify a single individual—and are also known as practice consisting of strong, well-known designers. Can you outline the thinking that went into the initial formation of the practice, even into the firm name? Was a collaborative method, or at least, a collective mentality, present from the outset?

**MB:** Pentagram was formed in 1972 as a partnership between five designers. Architect Theo Crosby had already been working with graphic designers Alan Fletcher and Colin Forbes in a firm called Crosby Fletcher Forbes. They in turn had collaborated with product designer Kenneth Grange. Mervyn Kurlansky was a third graphic designer who had been working with the other two. Each of the five already had a substantial reputation as a designer, so the combination was sort of a "supergroup." The story goes that stringing the five names together was simply too unwieldy and the name Pentagram was the practical solution.

However, I think there was always more to it than that. In the original structure, they made several key decisions. There would be no hierarchy. Each of the five would act as leader of an independent studio, each maintaining their own client relationships, hiring their own design staff, and operating as a separate profit center. On the other hand, all decisions would be made through consensus and that all five partners would get the same compensation, regardless of the amount of revenue each had brought into the firm. So from the start there was this sort of tension between independence and collectivism. Being individually accountable keeps the pressure on each partner to succeed. Sharing decisions and revenue keeps it in each person's interest to help the group do well.

This was all set up when I was in the ninth grade. It turned out the system was scalable (there could be more than five partners) and expandable (there could be additional offices). Today we have nineteen partners in five offices. Two of the original five have passed away, the other three have retired. Our newest partner wasn't even born when Pentagram was set up. Yet the basic set of structural principles is still scrupulously maintained. Not having anyone's name on the door means that any of the nineteen partners, even the newest, can represent themselves to the world as the key person in the firm, and their office as "headquarters."

I am always struck by the ingenuity and elegance of the organizational structure and surprised it's never really been copied.

**SS:** I wasn't around at the initial formation of IDEO, but I can tell you a bit of its history. IDEO has roots in Silicon Valley dating back to 1978 and was officially formed in 1991 when three design companies merged: David Kelley Design, Moggridge Associates of London (Bill Moggridge's company), and Matrix Product Design (founded by Mike Nuttall).

People often ask what the letters I-D-E-O stand for, assuming that it's an acronym. Actually, IDEO is the hyphenating form of the word "idea," so it makes a great name for the work that IDEO does. I have heard David Kelley mention many times that he didn't want his name on the door anymore, since he found that clients felt that they needed "the name on the door" in the room to feel like they were getting the real talent … and IDEO has very much always held the perspective that the talent across the studio is what makes the work great. Humility, support of creativity, and a belief in collective wisdom is deeply embedded in IDEO culture. You can see that very much now in both the work we are doing and the ways that we are expanding. OpenIDEO is a great example of that—it's an open innovation platform we created to open up our boundaries and engage tens of thousands of people around the world to join us in creating new answers to large, social challenges. Ideas abound!

**PM:** With a by now long record of many and diverse accomplishments, Pentagram and IDEO hold an established place in the design culture. What do you think are the attributes that can be ascribed to the Pentagram and IDEO names, despite the range of work and the range of designers employed? How are those attributes maintained across the practice, across the range of design-

ers, work, locations … as the firms grow and attract more and different projects?

**MB:** Again, I think there's a tension between two opposing forces, one structural, the other a bias. Each time a new partner joins, it has to be with the unanimous support of all the other partners. This includes partners in other offices. So if the partners in New York are interested in bringing on a new partner, we have to arrange for that candidate to travel to meet each of the other partners in London, Austin, Berlin, and San Francisco. The objection of a single partner can effectively block a candidacy. Debating about new partners is basically the way the firm talks about its future.

On the other hand, there has been a strong historic tendency to go outside the firm for new partners. Of the nineteen current partners, only three came from within, having been associates of other partners within the firm. The other sixteen came from outside, usually ran their own firms, and had already demonstrated a capacity for entrepreneurial success. So in effect we're combining the tendency towards stasis that any self-ratifying group tends to exhibit with the disruptive potential of clashing cultures. Each new partner is seen by all the existing partners as somehow being "right for Pentagram" yet once they join things inevitably don't work out exactly as planned. So each new member changes the overall group and is changed by it.

Even my partners tend to disagree about exactly what makes a Pentagram partner a Pentagram partner. The characteristics that are mentioned most often are a dedication to both the craft of design and to its larger potential as a social force; a skepticism about style as an end in itself; an entrepreneurial spirit; a dedication to ideas as the motivating force behind the making of form; and a conviction that the definition of design is always worth expanding.

**SS:** Culture is definitely the most important factor in what allows IDEO to thrive. There are many reflections on this, statements like "build to think," "fail early to succeed sooner," and "ask forgiveness instead of permission." You'll hear many IDEOers saying these things, and often when we are helping other organizations build cultures of innovation we will use these shorthands for

Collaboration at IDEO Chicago

much deeper concepts. But I do think there are underlying ideas which unite IDEO across the globe and across our evolution over time. For instance:

OPTIMISM. Given the work that we do, you must—must!—believe that a new future is possible. If our job is to innovate, we will never know the answer when we begin our work. That's a pretty scary reality to face project after project, year after year. Baked into IDEO's culture is the reinforcing belief that we can create powerful new solutions for our clients and their stakeholders.

PROCESS. IDEO doesn't define itself by any particular design craft, we employ designers of all types on varying challenges. The one thing we have in common is process. Much has been written about IDEO's process, and we've even adapted it for different audiences—social entrepreneurs and educators, for instance. Our belief is that having a process helps give you the confidence to address new challenges that come to you. That has been IDEO's key to growth. When we're asked to, say, help design the strategy for a new government agency, or build a system of schools to be affordable, scalable, and excellent… we reply with "Sure! We can do that!" … because we trust that our methods, perspectives, and talent will get us there.

EMERGENCE. IDEO recognizes that its growth and evolution will come from the ideas and enthusiasm of its people. We encourage a thousand flowers to bloom to see what grows, rather than centrally define strategy. The percolating of hundreds of designers creates a very exciting environment, and has extended IDEO in phenomenal ways—OpenIDEO, our ever-growing portfolio of work helping to improve education, our new non-profit IDEO.org helping to alleviate poverty through design, many of our newest studios around the globe … all of these examples and many more have emerged from the interests of our talented teams.

TOGETHERNESS. Collaboration is a great word, and definitely reflects how we work at IDEO. But there's something deeper behind our collaboration, I think. It's the realization that we're all in it together. That we know we can't get to new, relevant solutions on our own. That we need each other to stay inspired, to elevate our work, to create greater impact in the world around us. David Kelley often says that he started his own firm because he wanted to work with his friends. That spirit is profoundly embedded in the culture of IDEO. I definitely feel like I have six hundred friends across the globe, and we're all in it together.

**PM:** How would you describe the Pentagram and IDEO approaches, or understandings, of the concepts of teamwork and collaboration? Relative to the parallel ideas of individual authorship, or even design leadership, what role does teamwork and collaboration play in the conception and realization of a typical Pentagram/IDEO project? If it is a central value or method, how is it encouraged, or nurtured or reinforced? Are there incentives to an emphasis on such approaches—but are there also disadvantages?

**MB:** The promise of collaboration was a driver from the start, and I think that some of the founding partners would say that that promise was never quite fulfilled as expected. Because there is no managing director in a position to put partners and teams together on projects, it's up to the partners to initiate collaborations. It happens most often when a partner in one discipline needs the help of a partner in another discipline, or when a project is so big that partners can divide up the scope and work in parallel. Still, for each scope area, the work will be clearly led by an individual partner. We'll also come together when a client needs support, say, in both the US and Europe. The work will play out the same way.

That said, each of our big offices is essentially open plan: the partners all sit together in one common area, and the designers all sit together in groups by partner. That

Concept posters for the new Mohawk identity.

means that everyone can help everyone else. Sometimes I'll just turn in my chair and ask one of my partners for the name of a good photographer in Seattle. Sometimes one of them will see something my team is working on and come up and make a great suggestion. This happens all day long, and the work is better for it.

Not only do we not have managing directors to orchestrate the partners' activity, we don't have account executives to maintain the client relationships. If you're looking for disadvantages in the system, one is that this lack of hierarchical control has made us unsuitable for taking on really large jobs as a matter of course. The individual figure of the partner and the scale of his or her own team (which is small, almost always less than ten people) tends to define the project type. So there are only so many projects any one partner, or any one team, can manage. We "push the kitchen tables together," in effect, but that's different from commoditizing the kind of service we provide. I suspect any smart management consultant could double our revenue by setting up a management superstructure over the teams and bringing in a bunch of good client handlers. However, most of the partners would quit. We all like to think we don't have a boss.

**SS:** Based on my comments so far, you can probably tell that teamwork and collaboration are the lifeblood of IDEO. I often joke that nowadays I have no idea what I'm thinking if other people aren't around! All of our work—from business development to team building to doing projects to making sense of our learnings beyond the individual project to incubating new offerings—happens in a collaborative fashion.

We don't have dedicated teams for specific areas of focus as many companies do; there's often an adjustment as people begin working here. They learn quickly that there's not a "paternalistic" model at IDEO. Many of us even use air quotes when referring to our "bosses." Our model is designed for a different type of personal growth. You grow through collaborations, through intersections with different people, different ideas, different questions, and different perspectives. You collect these inputs and experiences and synthesize your vision of you, your place, and your path. It's a deeply networked philosophy, and your development happens through the many connections you have across the network. What's amazing to see over time, is that as a result of all of this pinging around the network, the whole system grows. We all keep getting smarter, as does the organization. Of course, this isn't without some degree of anxiety. It challenges many of our notions of growth, many of our family structures and educational experiences have encouraged a much more hierarchical dynamic. At IDEO, you are often facing your own responsibility in your work and your growth. Most of the time, that's incredibly exciting. There is one big disadvantage to this highly collaborative environment: scheduling! Aligning all of the people you want around you can be a very complicated endeavor! And having the time to participate in everything you'd like to do is challenging. But, as you can imagine, we're always designing new tools and processes for that …

**PM:** You both also hold academic appointments and work with students, preparing them for professional practice. How do the concepts of teamwork and collaboration (again, relative to individual authorship and design leadership) enter into your discussions with students? Can such approaches and attitudes be taught and learned, and if so how?

**MB:** I find that students today are naturally inclined towards collaboration. I'm not sure why this is. It may have something to do with technology: when you're working in an environment that is fundamentally connected and potentially impersonal—and the digital world is both—the hard borders of individual control and individual authorship seem much less important. Still, people are individuals, and I'm always surprised and slightly amused when I meet people in the world of practice who extol the virtues of collaboration while obviously presenting themselves as unabashed egomaniacs. I've always liked that Pentagram was honest about being both.

**SS:** This is a *great* question, and one that should definitely be pursued more deeply. Most of our educational experience has taught us to value individual authorship. Not just design school—think back to your K–12 experience. Back then (and still to this day), collaboration was considered cheating! Creativity is often a competition, emotionally filtering out those who determined they were the "have nots." We give assignments in our schools where there are clear answers that end with right or wrong—asking learners to repeat known, quantifiable knowledge ... rarely encouraging diversity of responses and perspectives, or even working together to create new answers and new knowledge.
But now the top leaders at companies all around the world are declaring the skills they most need in their businesses include creativity, collaboration, the ability to deal with ambiguity. The future is demanding of us that we, all of us, engage with it to create new innovative answers to giant systemic questions—such as global warming, crumbling infrastructure paired with monumental scale urbanization, poverty, access to information … these questions require collaboration, multiple perspectives, diverse knowledge, and great imagination.
Absolutely, all of this can be fostered. It's in us as humans to be creative and collaborative. It requires some different structures (and values) in our education systems, however. There's some great work happening in many universities now to create multi-disciplinary centers where students are asked to work in teams around real-world challenges, to combine their different perspectives into new solutions. The d.school at Stanford is a great example of this. They combine faculty from across different departments into a teaching team for each class, and assemble students from different majors to make sure there's enough variety in the class. Amazing results emerge. Students learn new methods for identifying needs and addressing challenges, they learn to work together, they learn the skills they want to bring to the table, they learn deep information about the challenges they are working on … and they have fun in the process. The d.school has learned that this isn't without stress … these students have spent much of their academic lives developing their own work, and getting grades based on the priorities of the one teacher they are trying to please. So they actually have a psychiatrist on staff—the d.shrink—who helps students make sense of their experience.
There are some exciting examples emerging across K–12 as well. Schools are looking to design thinking as a powerful learning methodology and seeing the value of building the creative confidence in our youth. IDEO has been creating tools and training for teachers to help them build their own design muscles as well—teachers, after all, are designing every day. How can we help equip them with the skills and mindset of design thinking, so that they can not only design new solutions for their classrooms, schools, and communities … but also lead the revolution building the collaboration and co-creation skills in our youth. The talent is there, we just need to design the system to bring it out.

The Tektronix 1410, also known as a "green screen"

# Creating the Future (1964–1986):

How a Passionate Group of SOM Architects and Engineers Came Together to Envision Their Profession through the Lens of Technology

## Nicholas Adams

Nothing is more subversive to the established order than new technology. Old hierarchies of skill and experience are reversed; rewards that depended on traditional evaluations of expertise are reconsidered and reevaluated. Technology upsets apple carts. So it might have been as computer technology came to Skidmore Owings & Merrill. Instead the experience confirmed the founders' faith in teamwork and cooperation. The partnership, as described by Nathaniel Owings, sought the young and ambitious, and set them free to experiment: "we planned a partnership refreshed by new talent."[1] That said, the decade from the mid-seventies to the mid-eighties looked like the end of an era with the retirement (or death) of the first and second generation of SOM partners (Cutler, 1972; Merrill, Severinghaus, 1975; Netsch, Bunshaft, 1979; Hartman, Bassett, 1981; Khan, 1982; Goldsmith, 1983). But it also proved to be a period of innovation as SOM architects and engineers developed a series of much-loved graphic programs: DRAW2D (1976), DRAW3D (1977–78), DRAFT (1981–82), and SKYLINE/ AES (1987).[2] These programs and the people that implemented them mark a high point of collective invention at SOM. Working as the "Computer Group," and based in Chicago, the programs almost—but not quite—became the industry standard. How the programs fell short of achieving that status reveals two sides of architectural partnership, as well as the precarious nature of architectural teamwork and the difficulty of sustaining it over time.

### In the Beginning

In 1971 a report on computer usage in architectural firms across the United States read: "Many architects still think of the design process only in terms of a pencil, a roll of tracing paper and great personal energy. Others say that design problems involve too many unquantifiable variables for the computer to be of use."[3] The report's survey found only fourteen design firms using computers, engineering was their prime task. Ellerbe Architects in St. Paul, Minnesota, one of the earliest to take an interest in computers, described

usage as "98% in engineering application, 2% in Architecture." It was SOM's experience, too: computers entered through the Structures Group.

In the early nineteen-sixties E. Alfred Picardi (1922–2010), head of Structures in the Chicago office and Fazlur Khan (1929–1982) convinced of the potential of the computer for structural analysis, used computers at first to check complex hand-run calculations.[4] In the fall of 1964 Picardi hired G. Neil Harper (SOM 1964–68) to serve as computer consultant within the firm. Harper had a PhD in structural engineering and had worked for IBM, where he had been assigned to support SOM. Now at SOM he undertook the reorganization of the firm's accounting programs and the development of a specification program called AUTOSPEC with John H. Schruben (SOM 1955–69).[5] Harper encouraged the partners to purchase their first in-house computer, an IBM 1620 and taught FORTRAN to Khan.[6] With their new tool, the Structures Group worked on discrete problems that ultimately formed a library of solutions.[7]

In 1968 Harper developed a program for SOM called the Building Optimization Program or BOP.[8] BOP had its origins in the solution to a specific problem. When a developer came to SOM to develop a site with an office building, the design partner would send specifications to the Otis Elevator Company to calculate the size of the core. Weeks passed between the beginning of design development and the delivery of Otis's estimates. Meanwhile, though the design of the massing and the skin might advance, the delivery of Otis's estimates might require a redesigned core and reconfigured structural and mechanical systems thus wasting time and money. Harper obtained Otis's specification book and after translating the numbers to code, was able to provide accurate elevator configurations in minutes rather than the weeks it had taken Otis. A client, visiting with a partner, could present nothing more than the site dimensions before lunch and receive a series of possible configurations in the afternoon.[9] It was a relatively simple matter to extend the program to analyze other aspects of the building (stairs, circulation, relation to the Chicago building code) and using modular design principles, Harper could even provide some rough designs.[10] As BOP developed in sophistication it allowed a user to enter in as much information as was available on a possible project and search through many standard rectangular configurations to produce optimum cost results for each.[11] It was, nonetheless, a controversial program. For Bruce Graham (1925–2010) in Chicago, BOP came "close to revolutionizing the way we practice architecture."[12] For others, such as Marc Goldstein (SOM 1961–91) in the San Francisco office, and a great supporter of computer initiatives generally, it was "absolute nonsense"—the program was, of course, limited to relatively simple box-like office towers, a Chicago specialty.[13] Indeed, the development of BOP may be the origin of Gordon Bunshaft's growing disdain for office buildings: "I'm not sure office buildings are even architecture. They're really a mathematical calculation, just three-dimensional investments...."[14] Was he thinking of BOP or was that comment also a reflection of the appearance of a new investment-focused class of clients? The problem with optimization, as Kaiman Lee, the coordinator of computer services at Perry, Dean & Stewart noted in 1975, was that it offered "a strong temptation to over-simplify the [architectural] problem."[15] It was, however, a program that provided SOM with a distinct advantage over other firms.[16] Seeking to replicate that advantage in new programs stimulated further experimentation. In that respect, BOP set a pattern that the next generation of programmers at SOM would follow.[17]

Harper left SOM in 1968 and was replaced by Lavette C. Teague Jr. (SOM 1968–74). Trained at MIT (with advanced degrees in civil engineering), Teague significantly advanced SOM's computer usage and in March 1969 the partnership organized a meeting, the Appalachian Conference, to discuss the current and future status of technology in architecture and to focus the firm's computer activities.[18] In the early nineteen-seventies Teague and colleagues at SOM with computer training developed new programs: PLUS, a planning and land use program that helped investigate the feasibility of mixed land use projects.[19] Teague also extended the usefulness of BOP, making it functional above sixty stories and adding significant structural and mechanical options.[20] In 1972 Lavette Teague with John K. Turley and Michael Breitman, developed SARAPI, a program that maintained a data base of space and furnishing requirements for interior design and planning.[21] Computer activity consisted of a pair of people in each office responsible for this nascent field.[22]

**Computer Graphics and SOM**
As alluring as these programs were—and the profession

quivered with the possibility that some of architecture's routine tasks could be eliminated through the application of computers—they did not address architects' central activity: design.[23] And this situation seemed unlikely to change. In 1968 Harper assembled a group of experts for a book entitled *Computer Applications in Architecture and Engineering* and in its final chapter, "Coming Attractions," he tried to look over the horizon. Would there ever be effective programs for computer graphics? He was doubtful. "Despite the truly remarkable advances which are being made in some isolated experimental developments, the immediate future of computer graphics for office practice is clouded considerably by both technical and economic difficulties."[24] Within less than a decade those "technical and economic difficulties" would be solved or on their way to solution.

SOM was alert to these developments. An inter-office memorandum dated January 15, 1971 from Gerald Call in SOM's Portland office to Marc Goldstein in San Francisco (and circulated throughout the firm) described a meeting with Donald Vickers, a student of Ivan Sutherland, the developer of Sketchpad, one of the most important early graphics programs, at the University of Utah. For his PhD thesis Vickers developed an interactive computer graphics system using a head-mounted display and a three-dimensional wand. Worn like glasses, the system gave the illusion that the wearer was surrounded by three-dimensional objects. A hand-held wand allowed one to interact with the objects by 'touching' them, moving them, changing their shapes, or joining them together. One could even create new objects and add to existing ones.[25] "I feel," wrote Call, "that we should take positive steps to become more informed about . . . the headset."[26] In the same year the San Francisco office hired David Sides Jr. (SOM 1969–73), formerly at Rust Engineering with Teague where they had developed Critical Path Scheduling software. Sides had attended the Appalachian Conference (as a consultant) and then worked for SOM in New York, helping with scheduling of the Carlton Center, Johannesburg, South Africa. Now in San Francisco, he and Marc Goldstein had been approached by Art Paradis, then a student at Berkeley, who had shown them computer-generated perspectives of buildings and they invited him to produce computer drawings for a housing project in Davis, California, then on the boards.[27] Impressed, SOM entered into an agreement with Paradis's new firm, Dynamic Graphics to develop "software capable of displaying data in graphical form." The agreement was also to involve the creation of a topographical database for the San Francisco region and the payment of royalties to SOM.[28] SOM also added three new employees: Charles F. Davis III (1971–75) and Bill Kovacs

(SOM 1971–78) in New York and Doug Stoker (1970–89) in Chicago. In an effort to centralize SOM's computer activities the firm moved Davis and Kovacs to Chicago in 1973, creating with Teague and Stoker, the nucleus of a Computer Group.

## The Bigger Picture

The nineteen-seventies transformed the field of computer graphics. The laboratory experiments of the nineteen-sixties (hidden-line solutions, half-tone, and the rendering of solids) move into the mainstream. The publication of William Newman and Robert Sproull's *Principles of Computer Graphics* (1973) provided the first textbook summary of the field. Throughout the nineteen-seventies a succession of experiments provide greater realism: Gouraud shading (1971) and its refinement, Phong shading (1974), allowed the creation of the appearance of a curved surface; the development of texture mapping (1974) and its refinement by James Blinn (1976) gives images a more realistic appearance; the identification of fractal geometry by Benoit Mandelbrot provided a theory to represent irregular surfaces (1975). Hardware also underwent a revolution. In 1971–72, the Tektronix Corporation introduced a new "low-cost graphing terminal for business and scientific users." The new Tektronix displays (the 4010 and the 4014) employed storage tubes (direct view bistable or DVBT), commonly known as "green screens" for the color of the phosphor in the tube. Even though the only way to erase a line was to erase the entire drawing (and start over) the sharpness of the image represented a significant advantage.[29] At the same time Digital Equipment Corporation introduced the PDP-11, a minicomputer that soon became the standard. Connected to a terminal (even via a telephone line to New York) it became possible to work outside the frigid confines of the computer room.[30] The appearance of the Altair, the first desk-top microprocessor in 1975, marked a more significant transition away from large mainframe computers. Lower prices, greater capacity and flexibility created an entirely new field—useful for films (*Westworld*, the first film to use computer graphics appeared in 1972), for the successful development of computer games (Pong appeared in 1972), and for architecture.

What an architectural firm should do about these changes was not wholly clear. In Chicago, Davis addressed the problem of SOM's business software—and left SOM in 1975, keen to return to architecture. Stoker worked closely with the Structures Group, preparing data for One Shell Square, New Orleans (1970) and formulating the Structural Generating System (SGS), later Structural Data Management System

(SDMS) used to run computations for the Sears Tower (1971). Developments in computer graphics seemed to suggest new areas for activity but gaining access to them was the problem. In 1973, Teague attended a conference at the University of Colorado, and reported to the partners (and those interested in computers) about a film he had seen made by a professor at Cornell University, Donald P. Greenberg and his students, that showed the development of the Arts College Quad at Cornell University through rough color images.[31] Nonetheless, despite problems of cost and technology, and the still-incommensurable nature of the new software programs that could not migrate from computer to computer, it was clear that computer graphics would take a greater role in the future: for now, however, his recommendation was to wait.[32] With the recession (1973–75) SOM let Teague go—he was a luxury in the absence of a mission— and with the departure of Davis, the partners appointed Doug Stoker director of Computer Services in Chicago in the fall of 1975.

## "We will bring them kicking and screaming into the twentieth century. Hopefully, before it ends." (Stoker)

Stoker's situation was slightly different from that of his predecessors. Harper had been, for all intents and purposes, the lone authority within SOM on computers. Centralization had only partially succeeded: Teague and Davis had a varied portfolio: in structures, specifications, planning, and finance.[33] Reflecting the changing status of work in computing, Stoker wrote a memorandum to Fazlur Khan dated April 13, 1976, concerning the organization and status of the Computer Group, then numbering five people in Chicago. His concerns centered on personnel—not just because he thought some of the members would soon be leaving—but because the work required of the group was "tedious and boring." To bring the group back to life he thought would require "effort from the partnership. We cannot develop systems without leadership and feed back from the intended community of users." He mapped out a team (three architects, an engineer, and an administrative coordinator) whose responsibility would be divided between maintenance of SOM's computer (PDP 11/45) and the systems that depended on it, and the development of an open-ended research agenda with the presentation of research papers, and the possibility of an "online graphics capability" as a goal.[34] Rather than using the computer tools available in the marketplace, he proposed that SOM should develop new ones. Fostering innovation in architectural practice was nothing new for SOM and the development of BOP had demonstrated the possibilities of innovation in computers.

Among those who must have been of special concern to Stoker was the architect Bill Kovacs (1949–2006). Although he had no specific training in computing (still a rarity in the nineteen-sixties), he had instinctual skills. He contributed to the SARAPI program and in 1975 (in Chicago) took on special responsibility for managing facilities for the King Abdul Aziz International Airport in Jeddah, Saudi Arabia. Jeddah was the most recent—and then the current—type of large-scaled project in which SOM specialized. It consisted of an air force base, a special passenger terminal to accommodate pilgrims for the Hajj, a royal reception pavilion, a mosque, a terminal for year-round traffic, hangars, a health care facility, and housing for hospital staff, police, and military. There were runways, service roads, a desalination plant, and parking for 14,000 automobiles. Though the project entered through the Washington office (far too small to handle it), the New York and Chicago offices expanded as they had in earlier times during the pushes to construct Oak Ridge and the Air Force campus. It was in this environment of intense pressure and experimentation, as the firm struggled to address the scale of the Jeddah project, that Kovacs developed DRAW2D, SOM's first graphic design program. He used a Tektronix 4010 with a ten-inch (diagonal) screen that only allowed the cursor to be moved by arrow keys. The command set was rudimentary: it had eight commands, Load, Save, Redraw, Add (Line), Delete (Line), Move, Rotate (or Copy), and Exit. For Walter Netsch (1920–2008), Kovacs used it to create a rough plan for the hospital at Blida, Algeria in late 1976 or early 1977 but was so frustrated by the process (and disappointed at the result) that he doubted computer-aided drafting would ever work.[35] Even so, it was the first step in the development of a computer graphics program and Stoker asked the partners for two new positions: one of which presently turned out to be Nick Weingarten (SOM 1977–85) who facilitated the next step forward.[36] Weingarten had studied with Greenberg at Cornell and had helped make the film that had impressed Teague in Colorado. While at the time every other film had been wireframe, the Cornell film used sixty-four colors and provided a glimpse of the possibilities inherent in the medium. Weingarten brought those experiences to SOM in February 1977.[37] Though initially assigned to the Structures Group, by May 1977 he and Kovacs had developed DRAW2D into a three-dimensional graphics program that became DRAW3D. Instead of the awkward Tektronix 4010, they used a recently purchased high resolution Tektronix 4014 (with thumbwheels for input) and a Calcomp 936 drum plotter that offered higher resolutions from multiple pens.[38] The new program had commands that allowed constructive geometry (Intersect, Mirror,

Array, Fillet) as well as specific point input (a radical idea at the time).[39] Though they had developed DRAW3D without any specific project in mind—just the sense that they wanted to develop something to "view and draw things," it soon found users.[40]

Projects and their diverse problems found their way to the Computer Group. Among the many architects assigned to work on Jeddah (they occupied an entire floor on North Dearborn Street), was Kristine Fallon (SOM 1977–84). Fallon recognized the massive time and effort it took to keep the hundreds of civil engineering drawings coordinated and approached Kovacs with an idea. Kovacs created a database to record the coordinates and prismatic shape for every building and paved surface. Whenever there was a major design change, the data could be updated and plotted at multiple scales as underlays for the manual drafters.[41] The Group also executed two-dimensional elevations for Graham (Pillsbury Center, Minneapolis) and three-dimensional high rise designs (the twenty-five-story 676 St. Clair, Chicago). They worked with Walter Netsch's studio on development of a three-dimensional computer model (Teaching Hospital and Housing Community at the University of Blida, Algeria, Tizi Ouzou) and on his "Late Entry" for the Tribune Tower Competition (1980). Each project offered new issues for their software. In 1978, the group solved the hidden-line removal problem while working on the housing at Mecca and undertook their first terrain mapping at Jeddah.[42] Some of the most complex modeling entailed studies of the tents for the Hajj Terminal where they invented a lofting algorithm to come up with a starting shape close to the minimum shape required to analyze structures with large relative deflections. In 1979 Mitch Green (SOM 1977–81), one of the architects working on 3 First National Plaza, Chicago (completed 1981) did a sun study of the saw-toothed building and the program was adapted to DRAW3D. A later sun study of the model of 1 Magnificent Mile, for example, proved that late afternoon shadows would not rest across the nearby lakefront beach.[43] Confidence in the tools opened the possibility of a new scale of operation. Bruce Graham's 467-acre King Abdul Aziz University, Mecca (1978–80)—one of SOM's mega-projects (unbuilt) was the first project undertaken entirely on the computer. Over drinks on St. Patrick's Day (1979) Fallon, now assigned to Mecca, asked Weingarten whether it might be possible to draft an entire project on the computer. With the equipment on hand, the answer was no, but Weingarten persuaded Stoker (and Stoker persuaded the partners) to buy a Xynetics plotter, more Tekronix terminals and build a special air-conditioned room, with the expectation of the delivery of a new PDP-11/70. A full drafting program was big change. To

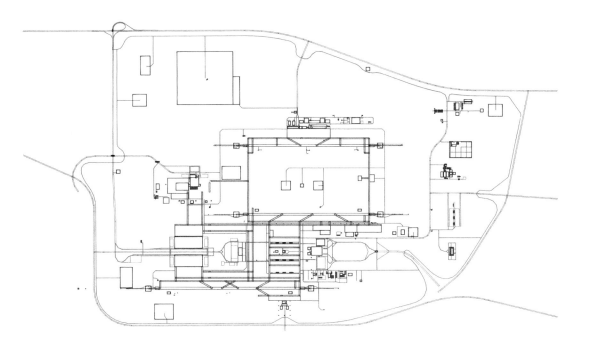

Jeddah, King Abdul Aziz International Airport, site plan, 1977. The plan contains mechanical and electrical distribution systems as well as transportation. The resulting data base coordinated more specific and detailed maps as well as area and volume calculations. (Computer Capability, p. 25)

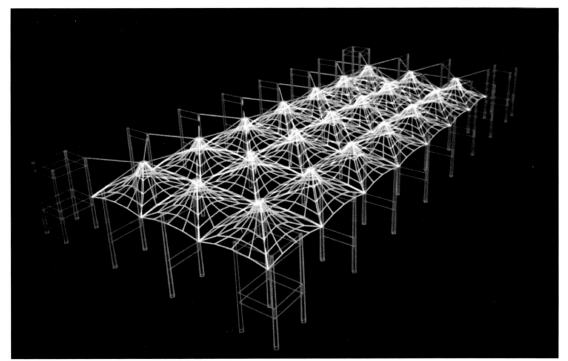

Jeddah, King Abdul Aziz International Airport, Hajj Terminal, 1978–79. Studies of the tents employed the first "lofting" generators for structural analysis. This later image shows a line of tents and their supports, probably taken from a Tektronix 4113 or 4115 terminal.

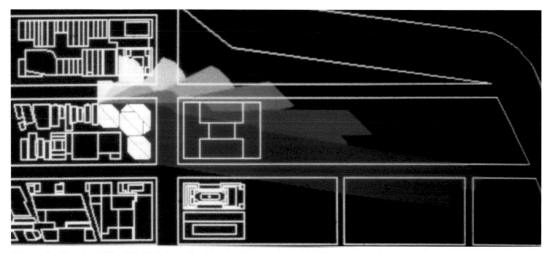

Chicago, One Magnificent Mile, 1979–80. Solar studies determined that even in the late afternoon the shadow from the building would not reach the curving lakefront beach. Originally plotted as a line drawing for Computer Capability, this is a later version.

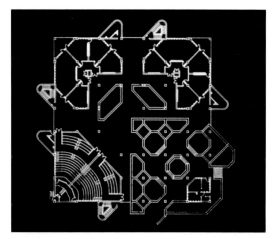

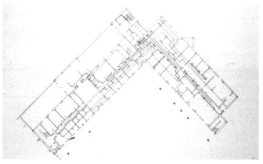

Mecca, King Abdul Aziz University, 1979. Plan of a portion of the academic wing with ceiling plan showing structural connections. The plan has been overplotted with mechanical ductwork (in rose).

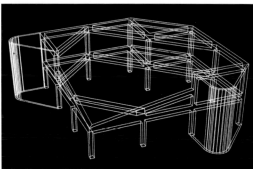

Blida, Algeria, Teaching Hospital and Housing Communities, plan and axonometric of a typical academic pavilion, 1977. The plan was developed using DRAW2D; the structural frame was developed in DRAW3D to help engineers and architects understand how to shape the beams to meet cleanly.

allow large data sets, Weingarten, as he did in the earlier version of DRAW3D, held the data in "virtual arrays" on disk, something that slowed the program but allowed an almost unlimited number of points, lines and symbols (blocks) in any one drawing. To overcome the menu and memory limitations, still limited to twenty-four commands and 16K of memory, he chained programs together, each with its own set of commands. This, too, slowed down execution, but it gave users a whole new set of geometric and viewing tools (CURV3D, MATH3D, etc.) while simultaneously allowing the program to connect to newly written application modules (MECH3D, STRU3D, etc.). Fallon became the liaison between the Computer Group and the Mecca studio. She met regularly with Weingarten to look through new code (often written the previous night); they would then bring it to

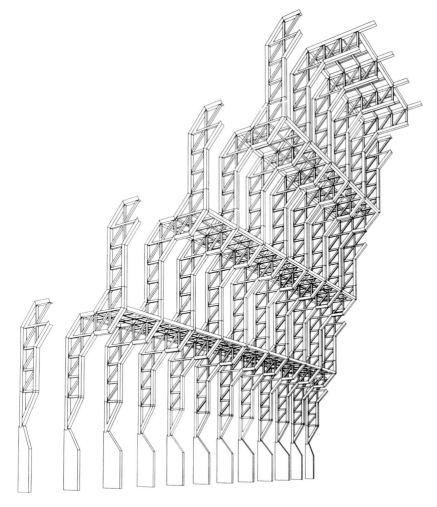

Chicago, 3 First National Atrium, truss, 1979. Two drawings executed at this time (a perspective and an axonometric) showed contractors how to run cat-walks and conduits through the space. The drawing also allowed engineers to test wind load, drainage, and safety. This image from Computer Capability provides some sharpness in reproduction (Computer Capability, p. 5).

the studios—working back and forth with the designers to refine the results.[44]

In one of the most unusual demonstrations of the new power of computer graphics the Computer Group prepared a scaled-up graphic model of Joan Miró's *The Sun, the Moon, and One Star* (1969) so that the Structures Group could design its interior structural frame.[45] Along with expertise and confidence, the Computer Group also gathered a library of Chicago urban sites and from that database one of their most dramatic productions was born: a graphic fly-through the city of Chicago with the major city buildings represented in wire-frame.

The presentation of the fly-through at the partners' meeting in 1980 was a turning point. Bruce Graham, after seeing it, had tears in his eyes and other offices requested fly-throughs for their cities.[46] The Computer Group prepared a brochure, *Computer Capability* (1980), that documented their achievements and that would serve as advertising for their skills, both within the firm and without. Stoker also prepared an assessment of computer usage and a plan for the Group. He evaluated current usage as: structural engineering, forty-five percent; mechanical engineering, twenty percent; computer graphics, twenty-five percent; architectural applications, five percent; administration, five percent. But though architectural applications were still low (restricted to elevator analysis and pro-forma investigations) he saw architecture and computer graphics as the major growth areas. Most important to Stoker, however, was the place of the Computer Group within the firm as a whole. Where would this new technology live? Stoker argued that the twenty-four people

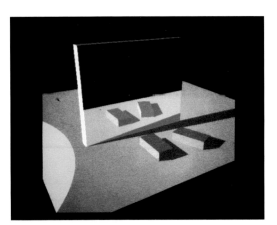

Brad Gianulis developed the first algorithm to create optical ray tracing, 1983. Ray tracing followed the path of light through pixels in an image plane to create reflection and refraction to create a high level of visual realism. This image was known as "Brad's Blocks."

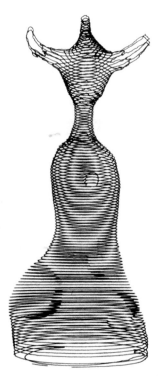

Contour sections of Miró's *The Sun, the Moon and One Star*, 1978. The maquette was CT-scanned, producing 120 sections that were output as raster images and then converted into wire-line images that could be plotted on the Xynetics plotter.

now in the group (defined by him as eight architects and engineers, three programmers related to financial management, five computer graphics specialists, six systems personnel) should not be treated as a profit center but as a firm resource, like the library or the typing pool. The group was, he argued, its own "design studio" (on the Chicago model) with members who could be loaned to other parts of the firm as needed. "The computer group personnel are charged to the job just as if they were a traditional architect or engineer. When not engaged in this activity, ongoing development or maintenance projects are undertaken within the group." This studio approach would allow the group to respond to needs throughout the firm, to advance what he called "the 'unique solution' philosophy of the practice." Stoker, still attentive to the intellectual stimulation of the work argued further: "Such an arrangement promotes 'pride of authorship' in the users, a better atmosphere for the training of designers to use computers and a synergism of ideas that will keep SOM closer to [the] leading edge of innovation." The Computer Group was composed of architects and engineers whose vocabulary

was architecture not system analysis. It was organized to solve architectural problems not oriented to create system solutions in search of a problem. In short, what had hitherto been a collection of people answering to Fazlur Khan, sought independent status as an applied research studio for the entire firm.[47]

By 1981, indeed, the Computer Group had successfully insinuated itself into SOM's major projects, either entirely or partially. Fallon took a key position as the liaison between the Computer Group and the studios, attending weekly meetings of the Studio Heads, the Technical Coordinators, and the Project Managers. In October 1980, with the opening of new work spaces on 33 Monroe it became possible to build little cubicles (two or three to a floor) where work could go on at terminals on the studio floor rather than in a single darkened room. There were critics and anxious architects, both on the studio floors and among the partners, but even skeptics would probably have agreed that computers had established a place for themselves.[48] At times, the novelties troubled traditions. Older employees (and partners) often did

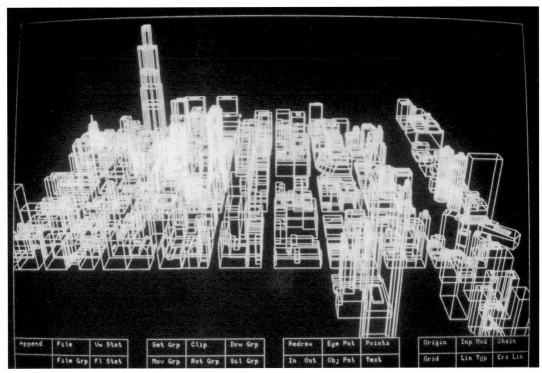

Chicago, The Loop, 1980. Screen shot of data in PLUS3D used for Chicago movie. Chain command linked this to other modules. Data was derived from Sanborn maps, a model of the city in the planning department and after-hours site surveys.

not know how to type or were raised to believe it woman's work. Computer operators sat at low chairs rather than the high stools customarily used by architects on the floor and some thought this a usurpation of status by youthful computer operators. "White-haired" construction managers were used to red lining construction drawings as they went along did not like being told they would get everything all at once.[49] And critics of the mechanical operation of the plotters thought they could never duplicate either the sharp-edged precision or the freedom of hand-drawing.[50] Late in 1982 Antony Mirante (SOM 1979–81) and Nathan Huebner (SOM 1978–81) replaced DRAW3D with DRAFT, the most advanced version of SOM's graphic software; its virtues ones that allowed it to become the firm-wide standard. This transition came as SOM was switching from the older 16-bit PDP minicomputers to the new 32-bit VAXs, which were much faster and allowed programs to operate in virtually unlimited amounts of memory. DRAFT took advantage of these technological changes but also broke with the on-screen menus favored by DRAW3D and most other CAD

systems of that day. Instead, it used a language based interface modeled on Chuck Atwood's earlier IPOL (Integrated Problem Oriented Language) routines. These were already used by SOM's Structural Data Management System SDMS) and Mechanical Data Management System (MDMS), and this allowed DRAFT to connect easily with the firm's architectural and engineering applications as well as with DBAS, the newly written in-house relational database developed by Dave Golter (SOM 1979–83). Despite a steep learning curve (it was like mastering a new language), DRAFT proved to be a flexible, easily extended platform for graphics development. It could be used to collect the design features of the entire building in two and three dimensions; it provided structural models that allowed analysis of steel-floor framing systems and provided models of the framing members; it allowed the placement of HVAC duct work and the insertion of plumbing and electrical lines; and ultimately the evaluation of lighting.[51] The compensation for having to learn a new language to operate the program was effective linkage between design and engineering programs at SOM and, in

Chicago, Inland Steel, detail. To create the effects of half-tone, Walt Bransford wrote the random dithering and Rich Rogers wrote "drivers" to draw half-tone lines and fill irregular areas. The Benson raster plotters could draw solid and dashed line, mid 1980s. The technique was first used for an actual project at the AIB Bank, Cairo. (Walter Bransford)

effect, greater creative freedom with the security that imaginative plans were also practical. Many who worked with DRAFT/AES claim that only with the development of the new Building Information Management (BIM) systems, has the software industry caught up to the place SOM's digital programs occupied in the 1980s.

An article by Steve Harrison (SOM 1974–85) in *Computer Graphics World* (1983) is the only published description of how the program worked in actuality. The building was the Pacific Bell Administrative Center in San Ramon Valley, California (1982–85), a massive two-million-square-foot office center for 7,500 employees.[52] Harrison connected DRAFT to DBAS to prepare furniture specification, estimate costs, create purchase orders, and coordinate installation in the building. Changes in design could be reflected in inventory. Harrison was enthusiastic about the way that the program allowed the coordination between the various disciplines and the way that wholesale changes could be accomplished from non-graphics terminals or using batch-mode command files. Even so, Harrison noted, it required a new staff organization. Job captains assigned drawings and completion dates and approved all changes; technical coordinators from each department acted as liaison with the computer staff scheduling terminal usage; computer programmers worked with the technical coordinators to insure that the programs

functioned appropriately and effectively. It also required architects and engineers trained in DRAFT; these were volunteers from the architectural production department. According to Harrison: "To create a corps of twenty-five users, trainees selection was based on potential ability, availability, and demonstrated enthusiasm. The average volunteer is about twenty-seven, and has been with the firm for approximately three years. After reading the introductory manual, trainees receive two-and-a-half hours per day of individual instruction for one week. This is followed by another week of self-directed study and experimentation, working with a technical coordinator."[53] It took about a month to train someone and because of hardware limitations only two or three people could be trained at any one time. Manpower needs required planning (and some expense).

In March 1983 Stoker presented a new vision for the use of computers at SOM. He noted the progress since 1980: nine new computers, thirty new terminals, and nine new plotters in the offices that had their own computing. Billing for projects was almost $1.5 million and the number of people in the firm "devoted full-time to computer related activities (not including accounting)" had grown to forty-seven.[54] Stoker now proposed that SOM offer computer expertise as one of its services. He mentioned companies (Tricad, Calcomp, Sigma Design, ComputerVision, Autotrol) that had been interested in

130

NORTHEAST VIEW OF BASE

HOTEL VILA OLIMPICA
THE TRAVELSTEAD GROUP

Poblenau (Barcelona), Hotel de la Vila Olímpica Hotel, detail, three-quarter perspective, showing the "wiggle," intended to duplicate the effect of a hand-made drawing. October 1989.

SOM computer applications to be marketed with their CAD systems. A hardware company (Gould SEL) had been interested in a joint venture with SOM to develop software for their work stations and clients elsewhere (Fort Collins Research Center, Oregon State Highway Division). In effect, he sought to make the Computer Group a revenue stream.[55] In early April Stoker described this concept as "The Design Workbench," a suite of utility systems developed by the Computer Group that might be packaged as a comprehensive design system for architects and engineers.[56] Doug Stoker was made a full partner in 1984 and a year later SOM began negotiations to sell DRAFT, briefly renamed SKYLINE, to IBM. IBM later renamed it Architectural Engineering Series (AES), one of its Architectural and Engineering programs. (Within SOM the program is sometimes called DRAFT/AES).[57]

The agreement to develop SKYLINE for IBM in November 1986 represented a triumph for the group. The sale brought money to SOM to support continued development and there was the expectation of future royalties. At the Christmas

party that year, the Computer Group rewrote carols to reflect their good fortune: "Skyline Sells" (sung to Jingle Bells), and "SOM is Going to Town," ("You better watch out/Our forces combined/We're making a product/We'll call it SKYLINE/SOM is going to town.") Yet the results over time were disappointing. In the opinion of some, IBM did not know how to market the new software and though SOM could write software for itself, developing it for others was an entirely different problem.[58] SOM's wasn't the only architectural software on the market, either. Perry, Dean, Stewart, in Boston, had also developed its own software and HOK had hired Nathan Huebner and Chuck Atwood from SOM to develop HOK Draw (1983). More typically large firms had purchased commercial systems (Autotrol, for example, sold software to Ellerbe and Caudill Rowlett Scott.) There was, in short, a market in architectural software. Even within SOM, the Houston office had already objected to the "imposition" of DRAFT from Chicago: the partners there wanted to use a software program produced by Intergraph.[59] Most signifi-

131

London, Bishopsgate Development, Exchange House, 1989–90. Executed on IBM RS/6000 Unix workstations, the original plan was to lay a raytracing over a photograph of the building under construction for an exhibition and book. In the end only the raytracing was used. (Nate Kaiser)

cantly a firm called Autodesk released a product entitled AutoCAD—one of a number of small scale systems—in December 1982 (two months after SOM switched to DRAFT) that opened architectural graphics to the smallest firm.

There were also economic problems. Even broken into modules, AES was pricey: between $22,000 and $35,000 for a minimum to typical configuration. Limited though it was to two dimensions, AutoCAD, the "word processor for drawings," cost between $1000 and $2500. AutoCAD ran on an IBM PC rather than the bulkier (and more expensive) RT required for AES. In short, a combination of marketing errors, misplaced ambitions, and the shift to the microprocessor dealt a blow to IBM's efforts to sell AES.[60] AES continued to be used routinely at SOM until the early nineteen-nineties and was last used for an entire project on the renovation the General Motors Renaissance Center, Detroit (begun 1996). The last use seems to have been in 2001–02 when Neil Katz, who began his career at SOM, in 1985, overseeing plotters in the New York office, used AES in preliminary designs for the new tower at the World Trade Center.[61]

## "The computer group was the people"

There was always something distinctive about computer users. Even in 1976, when it was only a handful, Stoker described the group to Khan as "a very tight, close-knit unit. Because almost all are single, we socialize during and after working hours much more frequently than other groups at SOM."[62] That was to remain the case as the group expanded. It was the spirit of the people and their time; formed in the shadows of the nineteen-sixties, a youthful cohort that had grown with the evolving culture of computer technology.[63] Here they were on the inside of one of the great American A/E firms and they had a chance to change the world. Unlike the studios that respected the older hierarchies more thoroughly, the Computer Group was comparatively open, the problems so diverse, the pressures so great, that anyone who could contribute was free to step forward. Under Stoker's direction collaboration was the norm and newcomers were welcome. "What I do remember most . . . is how especially kind and helpful everyone was to me, a little nobody, an operator with no computer experience whatsoever," recalled one woman.[64] Compared to the rest of the firm indeed, women found themselves more easily accepted and with special responsibility: Kristine Fallon was succeeded by Julie Rivkin (SOM 1979–91) as head of the users group (1984–87) overseeing the relation between the programmers and the studios and she was succeeded by Kris Stebbins Kelly (1987–91).[65] In New York, Natalie Leighton (SOM 1982–90) served a similar function and in Denver and Washington, the head of the users group was Louise Sabol (1984–90). Twenty years later people recall working within the computer group as the best of times—if not the best job—they ever had. They were on a mission. They had an unstuffy leader in Stoker. Members of the group remember his openness to novelty—revolutionary, as represented in phrases such as: "if it works, change it; if it doesn't work, document it." Paired with Weingarten, whose sharp programming skills set standards for precision and economy, they made an ideal team.[66] Collaboration within the group was a way to learn new skills; collaboration with others at SOM was a way to win over the firm. Collaboration was spontaneous. Walter Bransford (SOM 1983–90) describes the collaborative nature of the work within the Computer Group in a stream-of-consciousness recollection. If someone spotted a problem, the group rallied to solve it: "The plotting technology was applied to the Columbus Circle Competition 'Olympic Tower'—a Hal Iyengar creation of a tower hanging inside its frame. In a studio review some of us were asked to attend, Bruce Graham looked at some exterior view plots—six-plus-feet long!!!—and said 'that white background looks like

Designs for the tower at Ground Zero, New York, were among the last to use AES. This drawing was prepared for the 2002 Architecture Biennale, Venice (Neil Katz).

shit!' ... so I hatched this idea to make a graded sky tone from light to dark and hacked down the plotting system just to make these images. Tom Nelson and I stayed up all night nursing the final images at 1 plus hour each." Or on another occasion:

> Rich [Rogers] and Nate [Kaiser] and I were at the Ferris Wheel having lunch and Rich said something like 'how come we can't make design drawings look like they are hand drawn? Computer plotted design drawings look like crap.' He did the Rich Rogers ... laugh as he covered Nate and me in a cloud of cigarette smoke. I got the challenge. We agreed but we were booked up with the day to day. A few years later during some down time on the second floor I created this effect by perturbing the line equation parameters and the first 'hand drawn' plot was applied to a file of the fourth floor computer group space.... Later I did the same on the rasters of Nate's ray-tracings of Bill Baker's astonishing 'Building 11' in London.[67]

Stoker's advice to Carrie Byles (SOM 1986–) as she went off to London to integrate DRAFT/AES into the Canary Wharf project was just the advice he tried to follow himself. "Doug told me never to hire anyone who wasn't smarter than I was...."[68] It was a rule of which Owings would have approved. Seeking the best, Stoker presented SOM's experience to audiences in architectural schools and industrial settings across the country and abroad.[69] Though members of the Computer Group have almost all left SOM, some under difficult circumstances, they remain in touch with one another and cheerfully tell a stranger how much their time working there meant to them. Stoker and Weingarten are keen to identify correctly those responsible for programs that have long-passed into disuse.[70] Any discussion also turns to the protective interests of partners.

**The Lessons of Teamwork**

For many of the actors in this story, the key question about DRAFT/AES is why did it fail? SOM's switch-over to Auto-CAD and a cocktail of other programs took place in the mid-nineteen-nineties. But another question might be why it succeeded as well as it did? Was it just the times? The let's-do-it-differently attitude of the nineteen-sixties? The popular enthusiasm for computers? Or the presence of an inspirational manager? The support of visionary partners, like Fazlur Khan, and realists, like Bruce Graham?[71] Or the support of partners that combined aspects of both, like Gordon Wildermuth and Walter Netsch? Whatever particular combination it was, the partnership as a whole encouraged experimentation and profited from the collective energy of the group; that had been Skidmore and Owings's idea. Opening a breech in the routine, subverting a hierarchy and creating an environment for creative people to think and plan amid their day-to-day responsiblities, is no small achievement. Just because a founding partner thought it a good idea in 1936 doesn't mean that it can function the same way four decades later. Gathering individuals together for a common purpose is not a box on a checklist from Human Resources, but a balancing act that the partnership at SOM sustained at the highest levels around the introduction of computer technology.[72] "We did get work done . . . [W]e pitched in on helping architects move away from the tools they'd been using for 5000 years. But it wasn't just the hardware, the software or the projects. I think the story of the SOM Computer Group is the people."[73] For a decade, between 1976–1986, with the development of its major programs of design software, SOM was a partnership of ideas, staffed by talented people who worked with intense passion to "create the future." But SOM was also partnership in business so that when the economy worsened in 1990, when the advantages of SOM's own software over other products narrowed, when DRAFT/AES did not become the industry standard, the Computer Group as an applied research center was closed down.

Acknowledgements: I am grateful to many who indulged my curiosity in the Computer Group. In particular Doug Stoker and Nick Weingarten walked me (more than once) through the details of the programs they developed and the administrative hurdles they crossed. It is no understatement to say that this history could not have been written without their help. Both were prompt and precise in replying to requests for clarification and generous with documents. Kristine Fallon was an equally beneficent guide to the user groups and other aspects of SOM culture. Additionally I profited from the exceptional enthusiasm of former Computer Group members who chatted back and forth electronically about their time at SOM: Mark Andersen, Mark Evans, Mark Mulert, Walter Bransford, Peter Little, Natalie Leighton, among others. Electronic and telephonic communication with Lavette Teague, David Sides Jr., Charles F. Davis III, Eric Fishhaut, Steve Harrison, Neil Harper, Stan Korista, Jeffrey Heller, Julie Rivkin [Wheeler], Marc Goldstein, and Kris Stebbins Kelly, were exceptionally useful. Paul Gold unwittingly provided me with the title in a comment: "We really felt we were creating the future." I also met with Barry Milliken, John Winkler, John Zils, and had social conversations with many of the people mentioned above. At SOM I was helped by the managing partner in the Chicago office, Richard Tomlinson, who kindly sponsored a discussion of digital design (April 23, 2012) at the Arts Club in Chicago, and Carrie Byles, a director in the San Francisco office, who participated in that discussion along with Doug, Nick, and Kristine. Special thanks also to Neil Katz who first alerted me to the possible pleasures of watching a pen plotter and the brilliance of DRAFT/AES. Thanks are also due to Jayme Gately, Amy Gill, Jessica Gronfman, Pam Raymond, Eric Spitzer, and Karen Widi.

1   Nathaniel A. Owings, *The Spaces in Between: An Architect's Journey* (Boston, 1973), p. 66.

2   The actual sequence was DRAW2D (1976), DRAW3D, DRAWNW, PLUS3D (1977–78), followed by DRAFT (1981–82) and SKYLINE/AES (1987). (PLUS3D users typed in DRAW3D thus confusing names.) There is comparatively little literature on the development of architectural graphics in this period, but see Kristine Fallon, "Early Graphics Development in the Architecture, Engineering, and Construction industry," *IEEE Annals of the History of Computing* 20, 2 (Apr–Jun 1998), pp. 20–29; David E. Weisberg, *The Engineering Design Revolution: The People, Companies and Computer Systems that Changed Forever the Practice of Engineering* (2009), chapter 13, "IBM, Lockheed and Dassault Systèmes," http://www.cadhistory.net/ (accessed May 5, 2012).

3   Kaiman Lee, "Notes on the State of the Art: Computer Applications in Architecture," report for Advanced Management Research Conference, Managing New Building Projects, October 18–20 1971, p. 1.

4   In all likelihood this work took place at the McDonnell Automation Center in St. Louis. See Yasmin Khan, *Engineering Architecture: the Vision of Fazlur R. Khan* (New York, 2004), p. 56. Some of her claims for her father's early influence in this area require confirmation.

5   Harper initially proposed the idea of automating the cut-and-paste methods of specification writing and was rebuffed because SOM's computers could only produce text in capital letters. Ultimately Schruben warmed to the idea leading to AUTOSPEC. Harper, telephone interview, April 13, 2012. See also the comments of Schruben in "MASTERSPEC, In the Beginning," *SpecPress* 4, 2 (1999), pp. 1–2.

6   It is not entirely clear when SOM actually purchased its first computer. According to Walter Netsch, Khan encouraged the partners to spend "a million dollars" to buy a computer. Yasmin Khan believes this computer to have been an IBM 1620. This computer may have been a lease rather than an outright purchase, as noted by Harper (telephone interview, April 13, 2012). Doug Stoker, who arrived at SOM in 1970 remembers only an IBM 1130. See Khan 2004 (see note 4), p. 56; *Oral History of Walter Netsch*, interviewed by Betty J. Blum (Chicago, 2000), p. 127.

7   These programs have been preserved in the SOM archives in Chicago. Between four and twelve pages long and printed (or typed) on onion skin paper with titles like: "Moments and Deflections of Beams with Overhangs with Variable Beam Section," "Program to Check Stresses in Steel Members (A 36 Steel Only)," and "Wind Analysis of Multi-Bay, Multi-Story Frames" these item-by-item sub-routine programs formed the basis for professional papers by Khan and others. For example, Khan presented a paper on the "Design of Shear Walls" at the ASCE conference in 1965 on research related to the Brunswick Building. The program on which the paper is based is entitled "Frame-Shear Wall Interaction Program" (Program No. SO300)

8   G. Neil Harper, "BOP—An Approach to Building Optimization," *Proceedings of 23rd National Conference Association for Computing Machinery* (Princeton, 1968), pp. 575–83.

9   G. Neil Harper, telephone interview, April 13, 2012.

10   BOP had limited capacity for structural invention. Basically it configured plans with differently spaced columns.

11   Later it could even provide answers based on factors such as minimum initial cost, life-time cost, operating cost, and maximum return on investment.

12   Bruce Graham, "Computer Graphics in Architectural Practice," in Computer Graphics in Architecture and Design, ed. Murray Milne (New Haven, 1968), p. 25.

13   Marc Goldstein, telephone interview, October 21, 2010.

14   Quoted in Walter McQuaid, "A Daring New Generation of Skyscrapers," Fortune 87 (February 1973), p. 81.

15   Kaiman Lee, State of the Art of Computer-Aided Environmental Design (Boston, 1975), p. 18.

16   The number of buildings built using BOP cannot be counted. Basically, any office building built in Chicago from around 1968. 1990 entailed a BOP analysis. Other offices also employed BOP although less assiduously.

17   BOP was written in a problem-oriented language that architects themselves could manipulate without extensive training in programming—another model for subsequent developments. Harper 1968 (see note 8), p. 575.

18   We have only the sketchiest accounts of this meeting. It was held (puzzlingly) at the IBM Research Facility in Sterling Forest, NY and addressed the future of technology at SOM. C. David Sides Jr. kindly provided me with his report to the meeting entitled "A Transition in Architecture: Comments on the Development of Architectural Information Systems," March 22, 1969. The report reveals the fluid state of digital practices at this time.

19   See Niles O. Sutphin, William Sommerfeld, Lavette C. Teague, Jr., and G. Neil Harper, "Computer Systems for Urban Design and Development," Journal of the Urban Planning and Development Division, Proceedings of the American Society of Civil Engineers, 97 (April 1971), pp. 63–78.

20   Lavette C. Teague, Jr., and Douglas F. Stoker, "The Use of Computers in Preliminary Structural Design of Buildings," Computers and Structures 3 (January 1973), pp. 3–16.

21   In New York, Barry Milliken (SOM 1970–90) later developed the Hospital Space Programming System (1974) and with John Jaye, an Interior Design Information System (1975). Both programs developed out of the experience with SARAPI.

22   Thus, although there are personnel changes, in 1971 one finds: New York, Milliken, Charles F. Davis III (SOM 1971–75), Bill Kovacs (SOM 1971–78); in Chicago, Lavette Teague, joined by Davis, and Doug Stoker (1970–89); in San Francisco, David Sides Jr. (SOM 1969–73) and Jeffrey Heller (SOM 1969–71).

23   In reflecting on this period, John Winkler (SOM 1969–99) described architects as being ineluctably drawn to computers. "They would have used it to crack a walnut, if they could." Telephone interview, April 26, 2012.

24   G. Neil Harper, ed., Computer Applications in Architecture and Engineering (New York, 1968), p. 224.

25   Donald Lee Vickers, "Sorcerer's Apprentice: Head-Mounted Display and Wand" (PhD diss., University of Utah, 1972).

26   Inter-office communication, January 15, 1971, SOM Chicago archives.

27   David Sides Jr., electronic communication, April 26, 2012.

28   Letter from Marc Goldstein to Arthur Paradis, Dynamics Graphics, April 29, 1971, SOM Chicago archives.

29   The introduction of the 4010 culminated a series of earlier Tektronix oscilloscopes (564, 601, 611) that used similar technology. At a base price of $3950 Tektronix significantly undercut the price of CRTs from other suppliers. A low-end terminal from IDI sold for $11,000. See Don Bissell, "Was the IDIIOM the First Stand-Alone CAD Platform," IEEE Annals of the History of Computing 20, no. 2 (1998), p. 17. In addition the Tektronix did not require a costly framebuffer.

30   Computers generated a great deal of heat and had to be cooled down with air conditioning. Ignorance about computers was such that though the tour of the Chicago offices in this period conventionally included the "computer room," the guide would routinely point to the air conditioning unit and say: "That's our computer." Kristine Fallon, oral communication, April 23, 2012.

31   He also reported on computing at Perry, Dean & Stewart in Boston: even there, however, computers were still mostly used as a database resource and as a publicity tool.

32   Inter-office memorandum, Lavette Teague to partners, associate partners and others, "Report on Special Workshop on Interactive Computer Graphics and Engineering Design," July 18, 1973, SOM Chicago archives.

33   SOM's uncertainty about the status of computers is revealed in the tension between centralization and decentralization. Much time was spent debating whether accounting should be included among the Computer Group's responsibilities. Bringing it "in-house" might save money and might require the purchase of more hardware, both good things from the point of view of the Computer Group as it developed. Davis had worked especially with accounting. Stoker notes: "We were really paranoid about being labeled and evaluated like a normal IT department, but at the same time we wanted to control all the firm's computer assets. These two perspectives were mutually exclusive. The battle was finally resolved when the FMS [Financial Management System] applications were moved to a separate, and completely incompatible IBM system in the 1980's precluding any involvement of the computer group." Stoker, electronic communication, April 16, 2012.

34   Inter-office communication, Stoker to Khan, April 13, 1976, SOM Chicago archives.

35   Nicholas H. Weingarten, electronic communication, April 18, 2012. Kovacs left SOM in 1978 to work first for Robert Abel and Associates (1978–84) and then to found Wavefront Technologies (1984–94). He received two CLIO awards for his work on animated television commercials. In 1998 he received an Academy Award in the Scientific and Engineering category for the Wavefront Advanced Visualizer computer graphics system.

36   Memorandum from Stoker to Khan, January 19, 1977 SOM Chicago archives.

37   See Donald P. Greenberg, "Computer Graphics in Architecture," Scientific American 230 (May 1974), pp. 98–106.

38   There was also a large digitizing tablet, although apparently little used.

39   Weingarten's master's thesis addressed these issues. See Nicholas H. Weingarten, "Computer Graphics Input Methods for Interactive Design" (master's thesis, Cornell University School of Architecture, 1977).

40   Weingarten, electronic communication, May 3, 2012.

41   Kristine Fallon, electronic communication, April 19, 2012.

42   Fallon, electronic communication, April 2, 2012. Fallon presented the project at the conference of the International Union of Women Architects, January 1979.

43   The sun study program allowed the user to enter latitude, date, and time. It then positioned the view in orthographic mode from the sun's position. Anything visible was in sunshine; anything on the back or hidden by another object was in shadow.

44   Fallon and Weingarten, electronic communications, April 19, 2012.

45   See Oral History of D. Stanton Korista, interviewed by Betty J. Blum, Chicago, 2009), pp. 73–74, 77.

46   The Computer Group produced movies of the Dade County Stadium (1981), Washington, DC (1982), with Edmund Bacon, and an overview of nine cities (1984).

47   Stoker, "SOM's Computer Approach," undated [1980] report, SOM Chicago archives.

48   Fallon recalls that some architects thought that working on computers would kill their careers. Oral communication, April 21, 2012.

49 John Winkler (SOM 1969–99), telephone interview, April 26, 2012. Not all partners were equally enthusiastic. See, for example, Bruce Graham's comments about William Hartmann, *Oral History of Bruce John Graham*, interviewed by Betty J. Blum, (Chicago, 1998), p. 154. Charles Davis notes opposition from Roy Allen (1921–1992) and Walter Severinghaus (1906–1987) in New York.

50 The solution to both problems is interesting. In the case of drawing quality they built in acceleration/deceleration and pin up/pen down delays. Additionally a "home" function would return the floating head periodically so that the operator could re-prime the drafting pens. According to Weingarten there was also a plotter operator who mixed the ink based on the humidity of the day. The "Sketch" that gave the look of a line done by hand was developed by Walt Bransford in the fall of 1989. It gave the "snap" or thickness of a hand-drawn ink line. The first example used for a job was a representation Hotel Vila Olympica, October 27, 1989. (Bransford, electronic communication, May 4, 2012).

51 DRAFT could be customized to a special problem within a project or, in the case of the Layer Management System, adapted for an entire office. The Layer Management System, developed in New York (Barry Milliken and John Jaye, allowed the automatic repetition of plan details between floors. This New York variation remediated the separation between design and technical departments. Paul Gold (SOM 1980–90), telephone interview, April 30, 2012. There was a degree of rivalry between New York and Chicago in the area of computer technology, as in other things. Winkler, oral communication, May 3, 2012.

52 Steve Harrison, "Coordinating A/E/C CAD," *Computer Graphics World* 6 (November 1983), pp. 35–38. See also Nicholas H. Weingarten, "The Three Laws of Computer Management," *Inland Architect* (July/August 1983). pp. 9–12. Weingarten highlights some of the (unexpected) consequences of computer development.

53 Harrison 1983, p. 37.

54 Billing for this new service was not simple. Typically the Computer Group charged the design studio for computer time and storage. In some instances these charges were passed on to the client, in some cases not.

55 Stoker, "The Computer Discipline: Directions for the 80s," March 1983, SOM Chicago archives. Making the Computer Group a revenue stream may have part of the plan of Thomas Eyerman (SOM 1966–90).

56 Stoker, "The Microprocessor-Based Design Workbench: A Proposal for the Design, Development and Implementation of a Coordinated Hardware/Software Package providing a Comprehensive Design System for Architectural and Engineering Design Professionals," April 6, 1983, SOM Chicago archives.

57 Weingarten left SOM in 1985 (over the sale to IBM and SOM's unwillingness to develop a new paradigm for graphic software) to found Weingarten Associates. They merged with Evans Software Consulting to create Premisys, a company that later took over user services for DRAFT/AES. At SOM the new leader of development for DRAFT/AES at SOM was Eric Fishhaupt (SOM 1982–90).

58 Additionally, the software was more sophisticated than most architectural firms needed and priced beyond their means. A firm might (unreasonably) think that in purchasing a tool made by SOM that they would be constrained to design like SOM—or, worse, a client might think that if a firm was using SOM software they might as well move their business to SOM.

59 The issue was both one of quality and cost. The development of SOM's software was expensive and other Houston firms had started using Intergraph. A comparison test between SOM's software and Intergraph was arranged. In the end the 3-D capabilities of the in-house software won out. The challenge strained relations within the firm. Stoker, electronic communication, April 16, 2012.

60 A comparative analysis conducted by The Premisys Corporation, the company charged with program support for AES, found that AutoCAD was superior in speed, platform cost, add-ons and other areas of importance. To meet the challenge of AutoCAD by 1991, Premisys thought AES would need to be considerably upgraded. Weingarten, electronic communication, April 13, 2012.

61 Neil Katz, electronic communication, May 6, 2012.

62 Inter-office communication, Stoker to Khan, April 13, 1976, SOM Chicago archives.

63 Paul Gold recalls seeing one of the early programs for the first time in New York. An attractive young woman was sitting in a chair in front of what seemed to be a television screen. Recalling the moment, he describes how, despite the attractiveness of the operator, he was ineluctably drawn to the new machine! Gold, telephone interview, April 30, 2012.

64 Mary Patras Jewers, electronic communication, April 7, 2012.

65 Julie Rivkin [Wheeler] notes that that in addition to serving as beta tester for DRAW3D and DRAFT much time was spent in the studios reminding everyone "to save early and often." Rivkin, electronic communication, June 28, 2010.

66 "We all share the same feelings about them. Doug [Stoker] was the Daniel Burnham in his vision of the big picture, the opportunities ahead and his magic in pulling together the team. Nick [Weingarten], the Frank Lloyd Wright, synthesizing something so obvious, it belonged from the beginning. They had the touch. Geniuses. And real people. True friends of us all." Walter Bransford, electronic communication, April 26, 2012.

67 Bransford, electronic communication, April 5, 2012.

68 Carrie Byles, electronic communication, April 12, 2012. Stoker's aphorisms are still recalled by many: Have you written all known code today? Code! I want more code! You cannot be promoted until you can find someone who can do your job better than you do. A building is a 3D spreadsheet and we're gonna automate that. You just wasted six months in the past two weeks! We are automating the tools, not the process. Let's accomplish something in non-geologic time." Bransford, electronic communication, April 5, 2012; Gold, telephone interview, April 30, 2012; Weingarten, electronic communication, May 3, 2012.

69 Stoker lists some fifty events as panelist or lecturer between 1984–90.

70 Chuck Atwood (SOM 1976–82) developed IPOL and early structural applications; Mark Andersen (SOM 1981–91) wrote MEP software on DRAFT and AES; Mark Evans (SOM 1980–89) and Mark Mulert (SOM 1980–91) wrote early structural applications; Brad Gianulis (SOM 1982–85) developed the first ray tracing application; Rich Rogers (SOM 1979–84) and Walter Bransford developed architectural and Benson plotter drivers and run-length encoding to do shaded images; Larry Kearns (SOM 1985–90) developed a simple program using Layer Management (one of DRAFT's commands) to do area calculations at Canary Wharf. SOM in these years is sometimes characterized by the quarrels between its design partners. Compare, for example, the struggles over attribution at Inland Steel (Netsch and Graham) or Banco de Occidente (Graham and Smith).

71 Peter Little reported one form of support from Graham: "I was in Chicago from the SF office for a firm wide computer group meeting circa 1988 .... Bruce was in the elevator with a group of us. In response to someone's query about people who were resisting computers in the firm, Bruce calmly announced that they would be fired. I thought to myself 'there goes half of the San Francisco office.'" http://www.linkedin.com/groupItem?view=&gid=1794092&type=member&item=15300591&qid=3104fe86-2ba8-4848-9da6-8ce2024b5437&trk=group_most_popular-0-b-ttl&goback=%2Ermg_*1_*1_*1_*1_*1_*1_*1_*1%2Egmp_1794092.

72 One way to channel to the research impulse at SOM was the creation of the SOM Foundation (1981) led by Bruce Graham. Julie Rivkin Wheeler, head of the computer users group at SOM later worked to help fellows at the foundation with their computer needs (1987–91).

73 Bransford, electronic communication, April 5, 2012.

# 实践中的团队合作

彼得•马克吉斯

"实践中的团队合作"是由彼得•马克吉斯（Peter Mac-Keith）所发起的一个讨论，由 Pentagram 的主设计师迈克尔•贝鲁特（Michael Bierut）和 IDEO 的主设计师桑迪•斯派克（Sandy Speicher）参与，他们主要关注各自公司的合作方法和跨学科的设计实践。实际上，其讨论本身就是一个跨越设计文化的合作，其目的是为了借鉴那些不同于 SOM 模式的智慧，无论是实践的规模，或者是总体的设计特点。基于一个信念即建筑可以从其他的创造性领域得到更多的能量，无论是视觉艺术、文学艺术或是设计艺术，这些讨论是在一组设计或者其他相关艺术的团队的相对案例的研究——包括电影和动画制作、家具和工业设计、通信产品设计和战略性设计。

迈克尔•贝鲁特是国际咨询公司 Pentagram 的纽约办公室的合伙人之一，也是是网站 DesignObserver.com 的创始人之一，以及耶鲁大学艺术学院平面设计专业的一位资深评论家。而桑迪•斯派克则领导 IDEO 设计公司的学习领域，将以人为中心的思想引入教育的系统性挑战中。虽然她很多的工作主要集中在教育领域，桑迪在接待服务、通信、医疗保健和社会创新领域有广泛的领导经验和贡献。

贝鲁特和斯派克所引导的讨论产生了合作中所涉及的各个方面的挑战和价值，从"无签名"实践的观念到团队合作在全公司范围内的文化发展。贝鲁特观察到在 Pentagram 的公司结构和作品中的创造性的"独立与集体主义之间的张力"，而斯派克则是坚持"谦逊、创造力的支持和在IDEO的文化中深深植根的集体智慧"；两种实践凭借这些方法和途径而非"门上的名字"而蓬勃发展。

PM: Pentagram 和IDEO的设计实践各有一个很有力的、简单的标志性的公司名字———一个公司的名字而不是被认作一个个体——andare 也被认为由优秀的和著名的设计师们所组成。你可以描述出你们公司最初的形成的过程，甚至是公司的名字吗？从一开始就存在一种合作的方法，或者至少是一个集体的思想吗？

MB: Pentagram 是于1972年由五位设计师以合伙人的形式而成立的。建筑师西•奥克罗斯比（Theo Crosby）已经开始在一个名为克罗斯比•弗莱彻福布斯（Crosby Fletcher Forbes）的公司里与平面设计师阿兰•弗莱彻（Alan Fletcher）和科林•福布斯（Colin Forbes)合作。他

们转而又与设计师肯尼斯•格兰奇（Kenneth Grange）合作。默文•兰斯基（Mervyn Kurlansky）是第三个与其他两个合作的平面设计师。作为一个独立的设计师，这五个中的每一个都有了一定的声誉，所以这种组合是一种所谓的"超级组合"。将这五个名字简单地串联在一起显得太奇怪了，而 Pentagram 这个名字则是可行的解决方案。

不过，我觉得有更多值得一说的。在其原来的结构上他们作出了一些重要的决定。公司将不会有层级。五个中的每个人可以作为一个独立工作室的领导，每一个合伙人还保持他们自己的客户关系，雇佣他们自己的设计人员，而作为一个独立的利润中心。而另一方面，所有的决定则应该通过协商以及所有的合伙人将得到同样的收入，不管他们每个人对公司带来了怎样的收入。所以从最开始在个人与集体主义中就有一种张力。作为个人的责任，每个合伙人都有成功的压力。分享决策和收入使每个人都很努力从而使整个组合成功。

当我在九年级的时候这些就设置好了。这一系统是可以升级的（可能有五个以上的合作伙伴）和可扩大性（可能有更多的办公室）。今天，我们在五个办公室有十九个合伙人。原来的五个合伙人中的两个去世了，其他的三个退休了，我们最新的合伙人还没有出生的时候 Pentagram 就已经成立了。但是这一基本的结构原则则是严格地维持了下来。没有任何人的名字在门上，也就是说甚至是最新的合伙人，都可以向世界代表公司作为核心人物，以及将他的办公室作为"总部"。

我总是惊叹于这一组织结构的智慧和精致，而非常吃惊它从来没有真正被复制过。

SS: IDEO 最初形成时我还不在，但我可以告诉你一些它的历史。IDEO 的成立可以追溯到1978年的美国硅谷，并于 1991 年三个设计公司合并时正式成立： 大卫•凯利设计公司（David Kelley Design），伦敦莫格里奇联合公司（Moggridge Associates of London，比尔•莫格里奇（Bill Moggridge）的公司），Matrix 产品设计公司（Matrix Product Design，由麦克•纳托尔（Mike Nuttall）建立）。人们经常会问字母 I－D－E－O 代表什么，认为这只是一个缩写。其实，IDEO 是单词"想法"(Idea) 的连字的形式，所以这对IDEO所作的项目而言是个很好的名字。我听说大卫•凯利（David Kelley）多次提到他再也

不希望他的名字出现在门上，因为他发现客户觉得他们需要"在门上的名字"才能感觉到自己被真正的人才服务……IDEO 总是认为工作室所有人的努力才产生了很好的作品。谦逊、对创意的支持和对集体智慧的信念深深植根于 IDEO 的文化中。你可以看到我们正在进行的工作和我们正在发展的方式。开放 IDEO (OpenIDEO) 是一个很好的例子——一个开放的创新平台，我们创造它以开放边界以吸引世界各地数以十万计的人们加入我们，对大的社会挑战提出新的答案。数不清的想法和点子！

随着许多不同的成就纪录，Pentagram 和IDEO在设计文化中有了一席之地。如果不考虑作品以及聘用的设计师，你认为可以归因于 Pentagram 和IDEO名字吗？当公司成长和吸引越来越多的不同项目时，这些价值是如何跨越了不同设计师、作品、地点……而保持一致的？

MB：此外，我觉得有两股相对力量之间的张力，一个是结构性的，另一种是影响。每一次有新的合作伙伴加入，必须得到其他合伙人的一致支持。这包括在其他办公室的合伙人。因此，如果在纽约的合伙人有兴趣引入新的合作人，我们只好安排该候选人去伦敦、奥斯汀、柏林、旧金山去见每一个合伙人。一个合伙人的反对可以有效地组织候选人的加入。讨论新的合伙人基本是公司讨论其未来的方法。

另一方面，公司有一个强烈的历史趋势，即到外部去寻找该公司新的合伙人。在当前十九个合伙人中，有三个来自内部，是其他公司内部合伙人的共事者。其他的十六个来自外部，他们往往有自己的公司，并已经展示了一定的领导企业成功的能力。所以事实上我们结合了这种趋于平衡的状态，这种自我认可的组织往往表现出冲突的文化的分裂性。每一个新合伙人都被现有所有的合伙人认为是"Pentgram 的适合人选"，但是一旦他们加入后最后并不像完全规划好的。所以每个新成员改变了整体的组织而且自己也被其改变。

甚至我的合伙人都不同意到底什么才使一个 Pentagram 合伙人成为一个 Pentagram 合伙人。在这里提到的特点通常是对设计工艺的技术的专注，以及将其更大的潜力作为一个社会力量；对风格作为目的本身的一种怀疑；一种企业家精神；一个对设想作为形式形成的背后动力的专注；一个认为设计本身的定义通常值得扩展的一个信念。

SS：文化绝对是让 IDEO 成长的一个最重要的因素。对此有很多的思考，比如"为了思考而建"，"早一点失败，以便快一点成功"，和"请求原谅而不是被允许"。你会听到很多 IDEO 的设计师说这些话，但是通常我们用这些简略的表达方式帮助其他的组织创建创新的文化，我们会用这些简略的方式针对更加深刻的概念。但是我的确认为随着时间的推移，IDEO 在全球范围内有潜在的思想。比如：

乐观。考虑到我们必须做的工作，你必须——必须！——相信一个新的未来是可能的。如果我们的工作就是要创新，当我们开始工作的时候，我们永远不会知道答案。一年又一年面对一个又一个的项目，这是一个非常可怕的现实。IDEO 的文化增强了我们的信念，使我们认为我们可以为客户和他们的股东创造新的有力的解决方案。

过程。IDEO 本身并没有定义任何特定的设计技艺，我们聘请了所有类型的建筑师面对不同的挑战。有一个共同点是过程。有很多的文字描写了 IDEO 的过程，我们甚至将其改写以适应于不同的读者——比如社会企业家和教育家。我们相信一个过程帮助给你一个信心来应对所面对的新挑战。那即是 IDEO 成长的关键。当我们被问到，比方说，帮助设计一个新政府机构的设计方案，或者建立起一个价格合理的、可以扩展的和出色的学校系统，……我们回答到，"当然！我们可以做到！"……因为我们相信我们的方法、观点和才能可以使我们做到。

出现。IDEO 认识到其成长和演化来自设计师的思想和热情。我们鼓励不同的想法大量涌现，而不是集中地定义方案。数百名的设计师的想法的互相渗透创造了一个令人兴奋的环境，并将 IDEO 显著地扩展成——OpenIDEO，我们不断增加的设计作品改善了教育，我们新的非盈利的IDEO.org，其目的是通过设计减轻贫困，我们在世界各地的很多最新工作室……更多的这样的例子来自于我们的设计人才团队的兴趣。

团结。合作是一个伟大的词，绝对反映了我们怎样在 IDEO 工作。但是我想在我们合作的背后有一个更深的含义。我们认识到我们是一起的整体。我们知道我们不能自己达到相关的新的解决方案。我们需要各自使自己充满灵感，使我们的工作进步，并对我们周围的世界产生更大的影响。大卫·凯利经常说他创办了自己的公司因为他想和他的朋友一起工作。这种精神深深地植根于 IDEO 的文化中。我非常确定地认为我在全球范围有六百个朋友，而且我们都作为一个整体。

你怎样描述 Pentagram 和IDEO的方法，或者对团队和合作的概念的理解？与个人作为设计者的平行发展的思想相关，或者甚至是设计的领导地位，团队合作在Pentagram 或者 IDEO 的典型项目的概念化和实现中起到了什么样的作用？如果这是一个中心价值或方法，如何鼓励，培养或者加强？有哪些方法去鼓励强调这样的方法——但是这也有缺点吗？

MB:　　合作的承诺从一开始是一个驱动程序，我认为一些创始合伙人会说，从来没有如预期履行这一承诺。因为没有总经理这一职位，将合伙人和团队组合到不同项目，往往是由合伙人开始合作。通常是一个领域的合伙人需要另一个领域的合伙人的帮助，或者是当一个项目很大的时候，合伙人可以将其分工以同时工作。不过，对每个领域，工程必须被一个合伙人所领导。在美国和欧洲，当一个客户需要支持时我们会合作。这时工程也会以相似的方式进行。

这就是说，我们的大办公室本质上是开放式的平面：所有的合伙人都在公共区域坐在一起，而设计师们则是以组的方式和合伙人坐在一起。　　这意味着，每个人都可以帮助其他人。有时我会离开我的椅子而询问其中的一个合伙人，给我介绍西雅图的一个好摄影师。有时候，一个合伙人会来看看我的团队的工作，并提出一个好建议。这一切全天都在进行着，这样使得项目更加地好。

我们不仅没有总经理来协调合伙人的活动，我们也没有客户经理来维护客户关系。如果你正在寻找这一体系中的缺点，在这种缺乏等级控制的体系中，使我们不适合于非常大的项目。合伙人以及他或她自己的团队（团队非常小，通常少于十个人）往往定义了项目的类型。所以任何一个合伙人只会有这么多的项目，或者任何一个团队可以管理。我们"将厨房的桌子推到一起"，实际上，与我们所提供的商业化服务不同。我怀疑任何聪明的管理顾问可以靠设立一个团队管理的超级结构或是引入一组很会处理客户关系的团队，可以将我们的年收入翻一倍。然而，我们大部分的合伙人可能会退出。我们都喜欢我们没有老板的感觉。

SS:　　根据我目前的谈话，你大概可以看出团队和合作是IDEO的命脉。　我经常开玩笑说，当其他人不在的时候我在想些什么！我们所有的工作——从商业发展到团队建设到超越项目的学习——提供了一种合作的方式。

我们没有像很多公司一样关注于某些特定的领域；当设计师开始在这里工作会有一些调整。他们很快地认识到IDEO没有一个"家长式"的模式。　当提到我们的"老板"时，我们很多人甚至用手作出引号的动作。我们的模型是专为不同类型的个人成长而设计的。你通过合作成长，通过与不同的人、不同的想法、不同的问题以及不同的观点的交流而成长。你收集了这些信息和经验，合成了你对自己、对你所处的文章以及你的方向的看法。这是一个深刻的网络化的哲学，当你穿过这些网络中的很多联系时你得到了发展。随着时间的推移，人们很惊叹地看到，随着这一系统地改变，整个体系成长了。我们都变得越来越聪明，我们的组织也如此。当然，这也不是没有任何的焦虑，我们很多的家庭结构和教育经验鼓励了一个更加多层次的动态。因为在IDEO，你经常自己面对你的工作和成长。　在大多数情况下，这是非常令人兴奋的。

这个高度协作的环境中有一个很大的缺点：日程安排！安排你想要在身边的所有的人是一个非常复杂的尝试！而且有时间去参与你想做的一切是非常具有挑战性的。但是你可以想像到，我们总是在为此设计新的工具和流程……

你们两个也有教职而且都教学学生，帮助他们为专业实践做准备。团队和合作的概念（再重申一次，相对于个人创作和设计的领导）进入了你与学生的讨论了吗？这样的方法和态度也融合到你的教与学中吗，如果是的话，你是怎样做的呢？

MB:　　我觉得当今的学生自然地倾向于合作。我不知道这是为什么。也许和科技相关：当你在一个从根本上是相互联系和潜在的非个人的环境——而且数字世界——个人控制的硬的界限和个人的创作看起来不是显得那么重要。不过，人们都是作为个体存在，当我遇到有些设计师自己本身是毫不掩饰的自大狂，但是却颂扬合作的好处，我经常非常吃惊和感到有些好笑。我非常喜欢Pentagram对两者都很诚实。

SS:　　这是一个很好的问题，绝对值得更加深入地探求。我们大部分的教育经验告诉我们要重视个人的创造。不只是设计学校，想想你的十二年级的经验。回到那时（直到今天），合作被认为是作弊！创意往往是竞争，情感上过滤掉那些"没有创造力"的人。我们在学校给予的作业清楚地是对或者错——要求学习者重复已知的、可量化的知识……很少鼓励回答和观点的多样性，更不用说共同创造新的答案和新的知识。

但是，现在全世界公司的最高领导者在世界各地的公司都宣称他们的行业最需要的技术包括创造力、合作以及处理模糊性的含义。未来要求我们，我们所有人，面对重要的体系问题去创造一个新的答案——比如全球变暖，无法应付巨大的城市化的城市基础设施，贫困，对信息的获取……这些问题需要合作、多角度、多样化的知识和丰富的想象力。

当然，所有这一切被可以培养。这是我们作为具有创造性和协作性的人类。但是我们的教育系统需要一些不同的结构（和价值）。

很多大学中有一些多学科的中心要求学生面对真实的世界挑战，以团队的形式工作，结合他们不同的观点形成新的解决方案。　斯坦福大学的设计学院就是一个很好的例子。他们将不同部门的老师组合起来为每个班成立一个教学团队，同时将不同专业的学生组合起来，使整个班级有足够的不同类别。　惊人的结果出现了。学生学到了分辨需求和解决挑战的新办法，他们学会了合作，他们学会了技能，他们学会了面对的挑战的信息……他们享受这个过程。设计学院认识到这是没有压力的……这些学生已经花了很多时间发展自己的工作，他们试图在希望取悦的老师的课程上取得更好的成绩。实际上有一个心理医生－精神病医生－来帮助学生理解他们的经验。

也有一些令人兴奋的例子从前十二年级的教育中出现。学校正在寻找将想法设计成为一个强大的学习方法，而且看到了在年轻人中有创造性的信心。　IDEO　已经为老师创造了工具和培训，帮助建立他们自己的设计力量——老师毕竟每天都在设计。我们怎样帮助他们装备设计思想的技能和思维方式，所以他们不仅可以为他们的学生、学校和社区设计新的解决方案，同时也带领了年轻人建立合作和共同创造的改革。人才就在那里，我们只是需要设计一个将其发挥出来的体系。

# 国际现代建筑协会 (CIAM) 后的合作：
# 在莱雅蒙成的十人组

埃里克·芒福德

孤独的天才艺术家－建筑师像幽灵一样徘徊在建筑领域，性情恣意的建筑师把一切功劳归功给自己，以致于经常忽视他人的贡献。对很多人而言，这些特质与对现代建筑的偶像人物的看法密切相关，尤其是弗兰克·劳埃德·赖特 (Frank Lloyd Wright) 和勒·柯布西耶 (Le Corbusier)。与此同时，这一领域在设计规划以及在必要的建造过程中却总是崇尚合作。为了解决这个表面上的矛盾，曾经有过有很多的尝试，而在二十世纪六十年代左右，十人组的合作尝试提供了一个面对这些挑战的发人深思的例子。

十人组的合作发生在二十世纪中叶一个非常不同的实践环境，在当时1947年亨利·罗素·希区柯克 (Henry-Russell Hitchcock) 指出了天才个体和团队合作的关系。希区柯克强调了底特律阿尔伯特·康 (Albert Kahn) 工业建筑师公司的重要性，其为现代建筑实践设立了一个模式，即"公司的力量……不仅仅取决于个人的建筑天才……而是在于组织的天才，即建立一个极简单的快速以及完整的生产体系。"[1] 这样一个体系的目的是一个"好比由来自工厂的不同部分的机器部件组成的完美的共同协调，"然后在最终的生产线上组成为一个成品。

希区柯克将阿尔伯特·康 (Albert Kahn) 和"另一个伟大的建筑政府机构"田纳西流域管理局 (TVA) 之间相类比。田纳西流域管理局给予了美国区域规划组织 (RPAA) 的想象以具体的形态，对于分散的区域组织则是将新的水力发电的供电行业与郊区以及农村生活结合在一起。希区柯克认为在田纳西州橡树岭的设计中，这种建筑和城市发展的机构在生产组织上达到了一个新水平。田纳西州橡树岭在1943年和1949年之间规划的主要是由当时刚刚成立的 SOM 完成，[2] 它是一个有75000个防御工人围绕着第一颗原子弹的生产而组织的新城市。与阿尔伯特·康技术娴熟繁琐的建筑实践相比，SOM和其他的公司预示着战后建筑领域的未来，希区柯克用赖特的古根海姆博物馆 (1943年至1959年）作为例子，将其描述为"天才的建筑"。不同于基于"它们特别的便利设施的总和"的繁琐设计，这种建筑就好像诗歌和绘画取决于整体的影响。尽管画廊不是一个完全的成功（比如古根海姆博物馆的例子），但是这种由一个特定的著名建筑师发展而来的根本艺术概念，才是最重要的。[3]

尽管在二十世纪二十年代由勒·柯布西耶和德国"新建筑"(Neues Bauen) 的社会主义倡导者（比如，汉内斯·迈耶 (Hannes Meyer) 之间的争论为战后在政府机构和天才人物之间的冲突埋下了伏笔，这在二十世纪五十年代展开的辩论与早期的现代主义的强烈愿望完全相反。其逐渐被国际现代建筑协会 (Congrès internationaux d'architecture moderne/International Congresses of Modern Architecture) 的成员所清楚地认识到，在他们战后进一步努力地去指导新的城市格局的同时，却位于两个方面之间显得有些无力：一方面是身为国际建筑协会的偶尔成员但已经成为现代建筑公认的大师（路德维希·密斯·凡·德罗 (Ludwig Mies van der Rohe)，阿尔瓦·阿尔托 (Alvar Aalto)，奥斯卡·尼迈耶 (Oscar Niemeyer)，马塞尔·布罗伊尔 (Marcel Breuer) 和其他人)，而另一方面则是实用主义者，通常被大型政府当局所支持而设计高层或者住宅建筑。这一分裂的局面引起了建筑领域的严峻考验，体现在战后现代艺术博物馆将某些现代建筑师封为圣者，然而由罗伯特·摩西 (Robert Moses) 设计，却没有利用这些明星建筑师的才智的大规模的纽约住宅建设和基础设施。建筑学校，新闻报道以及展览惊叹于天才建筑师的各种游说，而西方工业城市和高度非殖民化的战后世界的住宅建设和城市化逐渐成为了建筑行业关注的边缘，而不是像战前那样作为关注的中心。

十人组的形成是为了努力应对这一新挑战，令人吃惊的结果是国际现代建筑协会的领导者将这一组织交给了一些亲自挑选的年轻成员。在勒·柯布西耶的领导下，他们选择了乔治·康迪利斯 (Georges Candilis)，雅各布·巴克玛 (Jacob Bakema) 以及阿尔多·范·艾克 (Aldo van Eyck) 来准备今后的大会。[4] 第九次国际现代建筑大会于1953年在普罗旺斯地区的艾克斯举行，为了指导国际现代建筑协会的全球性设计工作，大会计划发展一个新的"居住宪章"，范·艾克建议非西方的建筑与西方模式相比可能对未来有同样的有效性。他同时恼怒地拒绝瓦尔特·格罗皮乌斯 (Walter Gropius) 在此时对标准化和工业团队合作的号召，以及反对格罗皮乌斯对像范·艾克过去在国际现代建筑协会的同事勒·柯布西耶那样的"首席建筑师"的攻击。范·艾克和巴克玛同样反感他们眼中的新兴战后"体系"，其中美国消费主义与战后的军事统治直接相联系，这样使现代艺术无形的社会和艺术价值处于危险中。[5] 在艾克斯，这一共同抵制的态度来自他们非常不同的战时经验，与乔治·康迪利斯在法国北非热心参与的群众住房的问题出于共同的原因。这位在巴库出生的，希腊受教育的建筑师在当时活跃在阿尔及尔的法国复兴运动中，之前他曾与勒·柯布西耶一起参与的马赛公寓的设计中起到了一个核心作用，并曾经于1949年到过卡萨布兰卡以及丹吉尔，并与法国规划师米歇尔·埃科沙尔 (Michel Ecochard) 在国际现代建筑协会中一个被称作 ATBAT—Afrique 组织中合作。直到1952年，康迪利斯、沙得拉·伍兹 (Shadrach Woods)、弗拉基米尔·博迪安斯基 (Vladimir Bodiansky，另一个马赛公寓团队成员) 与其他人一起监督了很多在摩洛哥和阿尔及利亚的住宅和其他项目的设计和建设，努力致力于被博迪安斯基称作"大多数"的设计。[6] 在第九届国际现代建筑大会上，一个新的国际建筑协会的年轻组织的未来成员与新加入的彼得·史密森和艾莉森·史密森 (Peter and Alison Smithson，国际建筑协会的英国部分，现代建筑研究协会成员 (British CIAM MARS group)) 和其他的一些现代建筑研究协会的年轻成员，包括威廉·豪威尔 (William Howell) 和约翰·沃尔克 (John Voelcker) 达成了共识。[7] 史密森夫妇于1949年在英国的东英吉利亨廷顿学校竞赛中获胜后成为了英国崛起的新星，他们有着很严谨的密斯式设计，但是在他们在艾克斯划时代的国际现代建筑协会的网格展示中，他们开始尝试采用马赛公寓逻辑的巨构原型的城市组织，以及将其延伸到校园和城市区域的设计。尽管这一方向已经由勒·柯布西耶于二十世纪三十年代在阿尔及尔项目中提出，史密森夫妇的实践同时被他们对艺术的兴趣所充实，其包括了杰克逊·波洛克 (Jackson Pollock) 的作品，波洛克是纽约的抽象表现主义运动中的中心人物，还有欧洲艺术家比如米歇尔·塔皮 (Michel Tapié) 和让·杜布菲 (Jean Dubuffet) 以及以现代艺术为基础的伦敦独立组织协会中的埃德·保罗齐 (Ed Paolozzi) 和理查德·汉密尔顿 (Richard Hamilton) 的作品。史密森夫妇根据这样激进的方法去重新组织城市生活不仅仅是处于简单的形式主义。在第九届国际建筑大会中他们的多功能的伦敦黄金巷 (London Golden Lane) 参赛作品采用了网格表现形式，使用了贝思纳尔格 (Nigel Henderson) 格林街的玩耍的小朋友的照片，史密森夫妇的意图是在城市化中采用"人的关系"作为一个更高级的价值，而不仅仅是功能和技术的需要，不只是提供光、空气流通、绿色的开放空间和去工作的便利交通。他们并不否定这些国际现代建筑协会的价值，而实际上

史密森夫妇后来强调了他们与国际建筑协会和勒·柯布西耶的紧密联系，但是他们与战后国际现代建筑协会的塞特 (Sert) (他们所反对的) 相似，将现代建筑产生的住宅环境作为社区交流所需要的额外空间。与塞特不同的是，不同于埃内斯托·罗杰斯 (Ernesto Rogers) 以及杰奎琳·蒂里特 (Jaqueline Tyrwhitt) 关注于"城市的心脏"，史密森夫妇对第八届国际建筑大会所推崇的城市广场和传统的公共聚集场所并不感兴趣。相反，他们认为现代建筑师应该将流动的、非正式的、松散的相遇地引入并重新塑造城市环境。他们反对田园城市以及在紧接着战后曾经在1951年的英国节上展出的受到斯堪的纳维亚影响的英国建筑，希望恢复现代建筑战前的生命力。尽管他们自己无法实现他们在二十世纪五十年代早期的竞赛设计，他们却以地貌为基础的社会化的城市想法很快就改变了英国的建筑和住宅项目，比如由 J. L. 沃默斯利 (J. L. Womersley)，林恩和史密斯 (Lynn & Smith) 在谢菲尔德（1956年至1961年）设计的公园山 (Park Hill) 住宅项目，很多二十世纪六十年代的英国校园建筑以及伦敦的郡议会 (LCC) 的整个泰晤士米德 (Thamesmead) 新镇（1967年）和其他许多展示其全球影响力的建成项目。

早在1954年早期十人组已经在荷兰的多伦发表了他们的第一篇宣言，十人组的代表人物被要求于1956年在杜布罗夫尼克组织第十次国际现代建筑大会。直到1981年巴克玛去世，他们继续以十人组的形式在不同的西欧各地会面。[8] 他们关注城市化以及建筑师可以改变的城市形态的方式，这与国际建筑协会的初衷是一致的。但是与国际建筑协会不同，对十人组而言从来没有完全清楚他们的团体组织怎样起到作用，或者说怎样与城市结构相关的更大的客户组织相联系。除了对他们而言似乎是一个缩减的国际现代建筑协会，关注于功能分区、基本标准、原型以及立法程序，而十人组崇尚新的城市化远景。以这种方式他们扩展了柯布西耶的模型，即建筑师将一个创造性的城市远见变成了一个共同的愿景，其不仅仅与艺术相似，同时也与流行音乐并行发展。但是他们的愿望同样也使十人组成为一个新城市战略的智囊团，在某些方面与转变天才建筑师的建筑理想相矛盾。为了保持相对专注，十人组需要一个有着某种不同看法的政策，这一令人不安的方面明显地体现在史密森夫妇和巴克玛于1959年国际建筑协会在奥特洛的大会上对埃内斯托·罗杰斯 (Ernesto Rogers) 在米兰的托拉·维拉斯加项目 (Torre Velasca) 著名的反对上，称其为"不负责任的"。[9] 对十人组而言，埃内斯托·罗杰斯的错误在于唤起斯福尔采斯科城堡的历史建筑（1451－66年），用现代建筑与科技与传统文化形式来表达意大利的城

市生活。[10] 不采取这一意大利的 "新自由派"的方向，史密森夫妇、 范·艾克和巴克玛都希望保持建筑的真实性，根据他们观察到的城市工人阶级的需要来提供城市组织的新形态，他们通常使用原始的混凝土表面，而不浪费设计时间在复杂的饰面和装饰的形式上。为此，他们认为这一新的 "粗野派"的城市结构可以更好地促进社会的互动，以及为世界各地的日益混乱和令人困惑的战后的新住宅环境提供公共领域。

十人组的各种不同的积极和消极的方面可以清楚地在他们最至关重要的会议之一所体现，这次会议于1962年9月在前曾经是一个宗教机构后来被转化成了一个法国政府会议中心的莱雅蒙成修道院举行。 艾莉森·史密森、巴克玛、伍兹、约翰·沃尔克 (John Voelcker) 和瑞典英国十人组成员拉尔夫·厄斯金 (Ralph Erskine) 在斯德哥尔摩组织了这次活动，最初邀请了大概四十位建筑师，包括勒·柯布西耶、巴克里斯纳·多西 (Balkrishna Doshi)、丹下健三 (Kenzo Tange)、查尔斯·伊姆斯和雷·伊姆斯 (Charles and Ray Eames)、杰西·索乌坦 (Jerzy Soltan)、卢西奥·科斯塔 (Lúcio Costa)、汉斯·夏隆 (Hans Scharoun) 和路易斯·康 (Louis Kahn)。这些人物中没有一个参加了会议，最后大概有二十位嘉宾出席。参与者的确切名单没有被保存，艾莉森·史密森从发表的会议纪录中删除了一些出席者的名字。[11] 会议主题是建筑组织和基础设施之间的相互关系，以及在当时非常受关注的话题，新住宅项目和新的高速公路系统怎样转化了从伦敦到纽约的主要工业城市。由丹下健三1959年在麻省理工学院设计课程为波士顿海港设计的项目，他在当时将其发展成为1960年的东京湾规划，提出了在住宅单位和城市之间的结构关系的转化，对当时的世界产生了巨大的影响。[12] 他组织了新成代谢派（包括菊竹清训 (Kiyonori Kikutake)、黑川纪章 (Kisho Kurokawa)，槇文彦 (Fumihiko Maki) 以及其他成员），同时也开始延伸十人组对城市基础设施的想法。[13]

与史密森夫妇不同，丹下健三从二十世纪五十年代开始已经开始设计大型的城市项目，他和一些新陈代谢派的成员，比如槇文彦，与大型日本的建筑和发展公司联系紧密，这些公司积极地采用他们的设计建议，以很快修补日本战时的破坏推动战后重建从而使日本变成了除欧洲和北美之外的最发达的国家。新成代谢派的成员关注于可拆卸的和可以不断地被改变的预制元素，理论上进一步在伦敦被推进，于此同时，阿基格拉姆学派（彼得·库克 (Peter Cook)，迈克·韦伯 (Mike Webb)，丹尼斯·克朗普顿 (Dennis Crompton)，罗恩·赫伦(Ron Herron)，沃伦·乔克 (Warren Chalk) 和其他成员）很快展现头角。 阿基格拉姆学派的方法与史密森夫妇不同，

不仅仅在于他们受到巴克明斯特·富勒 (Buckminster Fuller) 关注轻质和高度流动性的元素的启发，也在于他们更乐意接受流行文化和高度扩张的二十世纪六十年代早期的城市消费主义。

许多阿基格拉姆学派的年轻成员也在英国建筑和发展机构工作；罗恩·赫伦自1954年起在伦敦郡议会（LCC）学校部门工作，他和乔克设计了圣潘克勒斯·斯塔克罗斯女子中学 (St. Pancras Starcross Secondary School for Girls, 1957年)。随后，他们与康普顿一起加入了军队（康普顿之前是哈洛新镇的建筑师，直到当时是现代建筑研究组织的成员弗雷德里克·吉伯德 (Frederick Gibberd) 的设计师）像十人组一样为1960年为伦敦郡议会的特别工程部设计了伦敦南岸中心。他们紧接着在伍德罗建设公司与彼得·库克合作，设计了很多其他的项目，其中包括了伦敦尤斯顿的大型重建项目，其设计团队同时也包括了罗宾·米德尔顿 (Robin Middleton) 和布赖恩·理查德 (Brian Richards)。[14]

在莱雅蒙成精心挑选的场地，史密森夫妇为了寻找在城市的尺度上概念化基础设施的设计方法去提供 "方法的模型"。他们的报告还包括那些以莫桑比克为基础的阿曼西奥·古埃德斯 (Amancio Guedes)、詹姆斯·斯特林 (James Stirling) 的莱斯特大学的工程大楼 (1960年)，拉尔夫·厄斯金 (Ralph Erskine) 为瑞典 Brittgården 设计的蒂布鲁住宅区域项目，以及由约翰·沃尔克 (John Voelcker) 提倡的英国西南城市的增长控制方案。[15] 接下来的是彼得·史密森夫妇的伦敦道路研究（1959年）的介绍，一个关于怎样最好地将新的公路基础设施与现有地城市肌理相结合的考虑，从而在一个特殊的区域内创造更强的城市特点的新感受，他将此定义为由噪音和主要公路的能量所限制的城市的 "岛屿"。史密森夫妇的介绍还包括了为 "公民的建桥"的相关问题，他们提倡在历史中心周围建新的停车库以及在周边建设一个新商场，使其避免穿过交通和过度发展。他们的设计图表中使人联想起维克多·格鲁恩 (Victor Gruen) 的作品，特别是他1956年的市中心的行人专用区方案 "一个更值得的明天"，但是却以一个完全不同的方式提出和讨论。史密森夫妇除了在高速公路的新时代关注于对集中的市中心的购物和办公的活力的保留，他们反对在历史中心建设额外的商业发展，呼吁保持低租金以保证当地小商业蓬勃发展，建议新的购物中心特别是超级市场收取高租金。[16]

实际上在当时与大型的建筑政府机构更加相关联的是康迪利斯-若西克-伍兹 (Candilis-Josic-Woods)，他是在二十世纪五十年代的法国周边的新镇和社会住房的大型建设的主要角色。[17] 与史密森夫妇对流动性和密集的商

业发展的影响的兴趣相似，在莱雅蒙成的沙得拉·伍兹 (Shadrach Woods) 展示了该公司为西班牙毕尔巴鄂附近的阿苏亚谷 (Asua Valley) 的城市化的参赛作品。这一方案与他们为1961年的法国政府设计的两个法国新镇项目的方案相似，卡昂—埃鲁维尔 (Caen-Hérouville) 和图卢兹—米瑞尔 (Toulouse-le-Mirail)，后者也在莱雅蒙成展示。[18] 阿苏亚谷项目要求连接五十个大型的，十层楼的住宅板式建筑使其成为一个新的城市组织，并用低层的线性的步行者以"促进"公共用途。在他们建成的图卢兹项目中，其目的是提供一个连续的步行者为本的城市发展的新形式，与战后开敞空间中的孤立的大众住宅高楼相对，被十人组定义为国际现代建筑协会的城市化的本质。伍兹相信"城市的结构不仅仅在于它们的几何形态，也取决于它们之中的活动"，而这些正是由"建筑和空间来表现和物质化，靠不同的路径和地点以及公共和私有的领域的连接"。[19] 在这一表达中，他指出了关键的问题是汽车和行人之间的"速度的调解"，而他的公司设计的私有的汽车行程是从"点到点"，结束了塔楼间的停车结构的尽头，而这像根一般的元素使行人的活动更加直接和自由。伍兹并没有将这些工程看作一个最终的总规划而是一个"规划的方法"的表达。[20]

其他十人组的成员以及邀请嘉宾在莱雅蒙成的介绍还包括了雅各布·巴克玛、吉卡罗·德·卡罗 (Giancarlo de Carlo)、何塞·柯德齐 (José Coderch)、斯特凡·韦韦尔卡 (Stefan Wewerka)，以及新成代谢派的黑川纪章展示的舱体大楼设计，后来在东京建成的中银舱体大楼，[21] 其在一个有争议的辩论中脱颖而出。这涉及了十人组成员阿尔多·范·艾克和史密森夫妇之间关于城市化本身性质的争论，范·艾克展示了他在阿姆斯特丹艺术学院教学时的两个学生项目，其中一个时由皮特·布洛姆 (Piet Blom) 设计被称作 "诺亚方舟"，是一个可以容纳百万人口的巨大城市设计方案，连接了阿姆斯特丹周围的六十个村庄，形成了一个由一万到一万五千人口组成的七十个村庄的"城市之间的整体"。每一个六十公顷的村庄组织了连锁的建成的聚集群，提供了一系列的城市功能，由一个四层的公路网络连接在一起。将交通的基础设施作为这一项目的基本部分，提供了基础设施和其内部建筑组的集合。[22]

莱雅蒙成的特邀的演讲者吉列尔莫·朱利安·德拉富恩特 (Guillermo Jullian de la Fuente)，当时勒·柯布西耶的设计合作伙伴)，黑川纪章、韦韦尔卡和格德斯都非常欣赏这一方案，但是史密森夫妇和沃尔克则是高度批判。范·艾克在他的演讲中提到莱昂·巴蒂斯塔·阿尔贝蒂 (Leon Battista Alberti) 的著名比喻，城市应该像一个大房间，每一部分都应该同时围合和开放。这些想法与范·艾克努力发展一个城市化的"成型的学科"相关，他不同意当时广泛接受的观点，即建筑师应该为政府住宅公司的匿名的理想化的客户而设计。相反，建筑师应该提供"城市室内的…建设相反的形式"以加强其特性，比如那些已经在世界各地的本土化的村庄和城镇，如马里的多贡或者美国新墨西哥州的祖尼斯。范·艾克将布洛姆项目看成这些想法的一个极好的示范，城市作为一个"构想出的多层次叠加的配置系统。"[23]

史密森夫妇强烈反对项目的重复性，艾莉森将其看成是一个"完全的法西斯"，企图控制未来城市发展的各个方面，从而结束了范·艾克的在十人组的框架内发展他的新城市化学科。另一方面，勒·柯布西耶和朱利安·德拉·富恩特则在没有建成的威尼斯医院项目（1963年）上找到了他们的主要灵感。[24] 在布洛姆项目的讨论中，范·艾克已加入了城市的城市／住宅的比喻，他提出了城市需要一个树木／树叶的结构，其树叶细致的组织反映在一个更大的尺度上即是树本身，或者正如他在其闻名的树叶—树木的图表中所表现的，"树是树叶以及树叶是树——住宅是城市以及城市是住宅"。[25] 作为回应，在维也纳出生，在剑桥受教育的刚获得哈佛大学博士的克里斯托弗·亚历山大 (Christopher Alexander) 指出一片树叶的结构和一棵树的结构不同，他当时正致力于在印度的农村的发展。在莱雅蒙成，亚历山大描述了他如何致力于量化在印度农村所需要的不同的功能需求，并产生了一个早期的以计算机为基础的方法在一系列相关的类别中去组织功能需要的模式，在莱雅蒙成会议后很快发表了《形式综合论》（1964年），随后发展成了一个模式语言的概念。靠使用这一数学产生的（尽管非统计学基础）的方法，亚历山大不赞成范·艾克 "城市不是一棵树"的观点，他认为城市不存在树一样的结构，但是反而可以被重叠的功能和文化的联系的半格的图表所取代。[26]

莱雅蒙成会议或许标志着十人组的最高成就，使其继续国际现代建筑协会在建筑师和城市化的关系的未来的考虑，但是其会议记录表明没有一个统一的协议存在。范·艾克继续对荷兰的结构主义以及对例如赫尔曼·赫茨伯格 (Hermann Hertzberger) 的作品产生了主要影响，但是这一方向与史密森夫妇和康迪利斯-若西克-伍兹努力重建城市工业社会的新巨构的最终努力没有共同点。但是这一会议和十人组以及继任的组织比如新成代谢派和阿基格拉姆学派也提出了一些在希区柯克的政府组织建筑和天才建筑师之间的新模型。在这三个组织中，许多成员当时积极建议，在某些情况下实施了一种与工业合作设计的新模型从而产生了新的城市环境。这也许不一定可以调和希区柯克所指出的建筑领域令人不安的局势，甚至到今天仍然没有被解决，但是这却是对建筑师而言唯一可行的方法，以避免明星建筑师的光环或者减少政府组织的标准化的影响。

1   Henry-Russell Hitchcock, "The Architecture of Bureaucracy and the Architecture of Genius." Architectural Review 101 (January 1947), pp. 1–3.
2   On Oak Ridge, see Nicholas Adams, Skidmore, Owings & Merrill: SOM Since 1936 (Milan, 2006), p. 24.
3   Hitchcock 1947 (see note 1), pp. 4–6.
4   一些其他年轻的国际现代建筑成员没有被当成十人组的一部分，包括 the British protégé of Jaqueline Tyrwhitt, William Howell; James Stirling; the Norwegian architect and historian Christian Norberg-Schultz; and Sigfried Giedion's son-in-law, Paffard Keatinge Clay.
5   Cornelis Wagenaar, "Jaap Bakema and the Fight for Freedom," in Sarah Williams Goldhagen and Réjean Legault, eds. Anxious Modernisms (Montreal and Cambridge, MA, 2000), pp. 266, 270–72; Frances Strauven, Aldo van Eyck: The Shape of Relativity (Amsterdam, 1998), pp. 223–30.
6   关于 ATBAT-Afrique 作品的背景，见 Jean Louis Cohen and Monique Eleb, Casablanca: Colonial Myths and Architectural Ventures (New York, 1992), pp. 301–63. 对战后的国际现代建筑演变成十人组的简要说明见 Strauven, 238–79. 对这一组织的第一个尝试之一的经典的描述的是 "Team 10 + 20," L'architecture d'aujourd'hui 177 (January/February 1975), 其中包括了 Kenneth Frampton 的重要文章，"The Vicissitudes of Ideology," pp. 62–66.
7   根据 Alison Smithson 和 Peter 在 CIAM 9 第六委员会的居住宪章与 William and Gillian Howell, Shad Woods, Aldo van Eyck, and Sandy van Ginkel (Alison Smithson, Team 10 Meetings 1953–1984 [New York, 1991], p. 19). 没有发表的 CIAM 9 的文件将第六委员会的 Smithsons 与其他三十位 CIAM 成员列举在一起，"社会问题"。这一委员会由三个 CIAM 成员主持，Pierre-André Emery, Georges Candilis, and either the Swedish historian and architect Gregor Paulsson, or the Swiss CIAM member Alfred Roth, and listed among the Commission 6 members Balkrishna Doshi, Fernando Tavora, Roland Simounet, William Howell, and Ernst May, but not Woods, van Eyck, or van Ginkel, who were on other Commissions at this meeting (CIAM 9: Aix-en-Provence, 19–26 Juillet 1953: Rapport des commissions, ETHZ CIAM archive, CIAM-42-JT-X).
8   Max Risselada and Dirk van den Heuvel, Team 10: In Search of a Utopia of the Present, 1953–81 (Rotterdam, 2004).
9   Oscar Newman, ed. CIAM '59 in Otterlo (Stuttgart, 1961), p. 95.
10   这一在 Otterlo 的讨论的更广的意大利背景在 Sara Protasoni, "The Italian Group and the Modern Tradition," 中讨论，Rassegna 52/4 (December 1992), pp. 28–32.
11   根据 Risselada and van den Heuvel (see note 8, pp. 99–101), 参加却没有列出的建筑师有 Le Corbusier's associate, Guillermo Jullian de la Fuente, Fernando Távora, Luis Miquel, André Schimmerling, Colin St. John Wilson, and James Stirling. Oscar Hansen 也被列出参与了 Strauven 1998 (see note 5), p. 397.
12   See Rem Koolhaas and Hans Ulrich Obrist, Project Japan: Metabolism Talks (Cologne, 2011), 以及即将举行的 Seng Kuan 有关 Tange 的城市化研究
13   Team 10 邀请 Maki 于 1960 年参与 Bagnols-sur-Céze 会议提出他的组织想法，与其他的 Metabolists 不同，更加关于不同的建筑元素被组成以产生总体的形象，而个体元素可以随着实践而改变，就如同在传统的本土村庄一样。见 Fumihiko Maki, Nurturing Dreams: Collected Essays on Architecture and the City (Cambridge, MA, 2008), pp. 31–32.
14   Simon Sadler, Archigram: Architecture without Architecture (Cambridge, MA, 2005), pp. 10–33, 45–46; Architectural Design (November 1975), pp. 682–83. Brian Richards 也与 Christopher Dean 一起参加了 Royaumont 会议展示了他们未建的 Euston station megastructure project there, "Team 10 at Royaumont," Architectural Design (November 1975), p. 682.
15   The Guedes, Erskine, and Voelcker projects are illustrated with discussion in "Team 10 at Royaumont," (see note 14), pp. 666–68; 670–71; 672–73.

16   "Peter Smithson: Team 10 at Royaumont," in ibid., pp. 674–75. 这些会议记录被重新发表有一些略不相同的插图在 Smithson 1991 (see note 7), pp. 37–97.
17   See Tom Avermaete, Another Modern: The Post-war Architecture and Urbanism of Candilis-Josic-Woods (Rotterdam, 2005).
18   "Team 10 at Royaumont" (see note 14), pp. 687–89. These projects are illustrated in detail in Shadrach Woods, Candilis-Josic-Woods: Building for People (New York, 1968), pp. 174–99.
19   "Team 10 at Royaumont" (see note 14), p. 174.
20   Ibid., pp. 684–86.
21   Ibid., p. 677.
22   Strauven 1998 (see note 5), pp. 372–75. Alison Smithson 在她和 Team 10 相关的刊物中没有包括任何 Blom 项目的插图，其原因至今不详。
23   Aldo van Eyck, Forum 3, 92; quoted and discussed in Strauven 1998 (see note 5), pp. 367–79.
24   本讨论和 van Eyck 的尝试的暗示去创造一个 成行的学科 的城市化影响的细节见 Strauven 1998 (see note 5), pp. 397–406.
25   "Team 10 at Royaumont"; republished in Smithson 1991 (see note 7), pp. 76–79.
26   Christopher Alexander, "A City is Not a Tree," Architectural Forum (April 1965), pp. 58–62, and Architectural Forum (May 1965), pp. 58–61. 第二部分连同注释见 Joan Ockman, ed. Architecture Culture 1943–1968 (New York, 1993), pp. 379–88.

# Essayist Biographies

## Nicholas Adams

Nicholas Adams is the Mary Conover Mellon professor in the history of architecture at Vassar College in Poughkeepsie, New York, where he has taught since 1989. He is a member of the editorial board of the Italian architectural magazine *Casabella* and author of *Skidmore, Owings & Merrill: SOM since 1936* (Phaidon, 2007). He recently published a short monograph on Gunnar Asplund (Electa, 2012), and is currently writing a history of Gunnar Asplund's Law Court Extension in Gothenburg. He has been a fellow of the American Academy in Rome and the Institute for Advanced Study, Princeton, and the Center for Advanced Study in the Visual Arts, in Washington DC.

## Eric Mumford

Eric Mumford is a Professor of Architectural History at Washington University in St. Louis. He received his PhD in Architecture from Princeton University; his MArch from MIT, and an AB in History from Harvard University. He is the author of *The CIAM Discourse on Urbanism, 1928–1960* (MIT Press, 2000), the only book-length history of the International Congress of Modern Architecture. He is also the editor and co-author of *Josep Lluís Sert: The Architect of Urban Design* (Yale University Press, 2008) and *Modern Architecture in St. Louis: Washington University and Postwar American Architecture, 1948–1973* (Washington University/University of Chicago Press, 2004), and the author of *Defining Urban Design: CIAM Architects and the Formation of a Discipline, 1937–69* (Yale University Press, 2009), as well as other works. He currently serves as chair of the Harvard Graduate School of Design Visiting Committee.

## Eeva-Liisa Pelkonen

Eeva-Liisa Pelkonen is an Assistant Professor at Yale School of Architecture, where she also directs the Masters of Environmental Design program and the Modern Architectural Archives Lab. She received her MArch from Tampere Technical University, a Masters of Environmental Design from Yale, and a PhD from Columbia University. She is the author of *Achtung Architektur! Image and Phantasm in Contemporary Austrian Architecture* (MIT Press, 1996). Her second book *Eero Saarinen: Shaping the Future*, which is co-edited by Donald Albrecht (Yale University Press, 2006), won the Sir Banister Fletcher Award in 2007, and the Philip Johnson Book Award in 2008. She most recently served as editor for the book: *Kevin Roche: Architecture as Environment* (Yale, 2011).

## Susan Szenasy

In 1986 Susan Szenasy was named chief editor of *Metropolis,* the New York City-based magazine of architecture, culture, and design. During her seventeen years as Editor-in-Chief, the magazine has gained international recognition and has won numerous awards. Susan is the author of several books on design, including *The Home* (Macmillan, 1985) and *Light* (Running Press, 1986). She is a frequent lecturer and panel moderator on broad-ranging design topics, and steers Metropolis's Conferences, including Wonderbrands, Wonderbrands West, Net@Work, Business UnUsual, Teaching Green, and Design Entrepreneurs.

# Juror Biographies

## Robert Diemer

Robert Diemer is the founding partner of In Posse LLC with over twenty-eight years experience in engineering building systems. In Posse is an independent environmental consulting firm headquartered in Philadelphia, focused exclusively on services in the energy and sustainable design sectors of the built environment. Diemer is an expert in the design and integration of high performance mechanical systems with a specialization in sustainable systems. He is the former Chair of the Delaware Valley Green Building Council, and has lectured extensively on sustainable design and high performance HVAC systems including presentations at Design on the Delaware in Philadelphia, the Green Building Design Salon in New York, and Light Focus at the Building Performance Congress, in Frankfurt, Germany. Diemer is an Adjunct Professor at Philadelphia University and teaches the Masters of Science in Sustainable Design, High Performance Systems course. He is a licensed professional engineer in New York, New Jersey, and Pennsylvania, a member of ASHRAE and is a LEED Accredited Professional.

## Einar Jarmund

Einar Jarmund is a founding member of Jarmund/Vigsnæs AS Architects MNAL, an Oslo-based practice also led by partners Håkon Vigsnæs and Alessandra Kosberg. Jarmund was born in 1962 in Oslo and graduated from the Oslo School of Architecture in 1987. He received a Master of Architecture degree from the University of Washington in 1989 and taught there in 1990. In 1992 Einar returned to Norway and established Jarmund/Vigsnæs Architects in 1995 with Håkon Vigsnæs. He has since taught at the Oslo School of Architecture, the Bergen School of Architecture, Washington University in St. Louis, and the University of Arizona. Noted public projects include the Oslo School of Architecture (2001), the Svalbard Science Center in Spitsbergen, Norway (2005), and the Norwegian Ministry of Defence in Oslo, Norway (2006).

## Oliver Schulze

Oliver Schulze is the Director at Gehl Studio, an Urban Quality Consultant firm based in Copenhagen. As an architect and urban designer, Schulze explores the relationship of urban life, urban form, and urban infrastructure to create inviting and stimulating urban environments for all people. He has worked on major city development projects across Europe, North and Central America, the Middle East, and North Africa. He won the UK's Civic Trust Award, CABE Special Award for Public Spaces, and Landscape Institute Award, for the New Road in Brighton project, in 2009. He was elected a corporate member of the Royal Institute of British Architects, and was also a founding member of the German Sustainable Building Council (DGNB). Schulze has lectured as a keynote speaker at many conferences, and has held several visiting professorships including University of Pennsylvania and Washington University in St. Louis. Schulze has been recently selected for the AC Martin Visiting Professorship in Architectural Design of University of Southern California School of Architecture.

# Editorial Board Biographies

## Luis Fernández-Galiano

Luis Fernández-Galiano (1950) is an architect, professor at the School of Architecture of Madrid's Universidad Politécnica, and editor of *AV/Arquitectura Viva.* Between 1993 and 2006 he was in charge of the weekly architecture page of *El País,* where he now writes for the Op-Ed section. A member of the Royal Academy of Doctors, he has been Cullinan Professor at Rice University, Franke Fellow at Yale University, a visiting scholar at the Getty Center, and a visiting critic at Princeton, Harvard, and the Berlage Institute; and has taught courses at Menéndez Pelayo and Complutense Universities. President of the jury in the 9th Venice Architecture Biennial, expert and juror of the Mies van der Rohe European Award, he has curated the exhibitions *El espacio privado, Extreme Eurasia* (in Tokyo and Madrid) and *Bucky Fuller & Spaceship Earth,* and has been on the jury of several international competitions, in Europe and America. Among his books are *La Quimera Moderna, Fire and Memory* (MIT Press, 1991), *Spain Builds* (MoMA, 2006), and *Atlas, Global Architecture Circa 2000,* a series of five volumes (Fundación BBVA, 2008).

## Peter MacKeith

Peter MacKeith is Associate Dean and Associate Professor of Architecture at the Sam Fox School of Design & Visual Arts, Washington University in St. Louis. He received his MArch from Yale University and his BA in Literature and International Relations from the University of Virginia. MacKeith directed the International Masters program in architecture at the Helsinki University of Technology from 1994 to 1999, and previously taught design and architectural theory at Yale University and the University of Virginia. MacKeith has worked in practices in both the United States and Finland and has written and lectured extensively in the United States, Finland, and across the Nordic countries on the work of Alvar Aalto, and on contemporary Finnish and Nordic architecture in general. A past editor of *Perspecta: The Yale Architectural Journal,* he is also the author and/or editor of *The Finland Pavilions: Finland at the Universal Expositions 1900–1992* (City Publishers, 1992), *Encounters: Architectural Essays, a selection of essays by Juhani Pallasmaa* (Rakennustieto, 2005), *The Dissolving Corporation: Contemporary Architecture and Corporate Identity in Finland* (The Finnish Institute for Business and Policy Studies, 2005), and *Archipelago, Essays of Architecture* (Rakennustieto, 2006). His analytical drawings of Aalto's buildings were included in the 1998 MoMA Aalto retrospective; he produced the St. Louis display of the international exhibition *Eero Saarinen: Shaping the Future*. MacKeith is the recipient of a Fulbright Fellowship, research grants from The Graham Foundation for Advanced Studies in the Visual Arts, and is active in both the ACSA and the EAAE. In 2008, he received a Creative Achievement in Design Education Award from the Association of Collegiate Schools of Architecture (ACSA).

**Joan Ockman**

Joan Ockman served as Director of the Temple Hoyne Buell Center for the Study of American Architecture at Columbia University from 1994 to 2008 and was a member of the faculty of Columbia's Graduate School of Architecture, Planning and Preservation for more than two decades. She is currently teaching at the University of Pennsylvania and has also taught at Yale, Cornell, the Graduate Center of City University of New York, and the Berlage Institute in Rotterdam. Educated at Harvard and Cooper Union School of Architecture, she began her career at the Institute for Architecture and Urban Studies in New York, where she was an editor of *Oppositions* journal and was responsible for the Oppositions Books series. Among her numerous publications, her award-winning anthology *Architecture Culture 1943–1968* (Rizzoli, 1993) is now in its fifth printing. In 2000 she conceived and curated a major project on Pragmatist philosophy and architecture sponsored by SOM, which resulted in a conference at the Museum of Modern Art and a book entitled *The Pragmatist Imagination: Thinking about Things in the Making* (Princeton Architectural Press, 2001). The American Institute of Architects honored her in 2003 with an award for collaborative achievement. Her recent book, *Architecture School: Three Centuries of Educating Architects in North America* (MIT Press, 2012) was released this year. She is also completing a history of architecture and the Cold War.

# Project Credits

**1 New Blackfriars**
**London, United Kingdom**
**Designed 2011**

Client: The Carlyle Group
Design Director: Kent Jackson
Senior Designer: Firas Hnoosh
Project Manager: Peter Jackson
Team Members: Firas Hnoosh, Timo Kujala, Christopher Wollaston, Kaiti Papapavlou, Albara Saimaldahar, Valeria Segovia, William Gowland, Omid Kamvari, Pedja Pantovic, Paolo Rossi
Structural Consultant: Bill Baker SOM Chicago, Stuart Marsh SOM London
Mechanical Consultant: Hoare Lea
Environmental Consultant: Hoare Lea

**Seoul Light DMC Tower**
**Seoul, South Korea**
**Designed 2009–11**

Client: Seoul Light AMC Ltd.
Design Partner: Mustafa Abadan
Managing Partner: TJ Gottesdiener
Structural Partner: Charles Besjak
Project Manager: Brant Coletta
Senior Design Architect: Basil Lee
Senior Technical Coordinator: Nicholas Holt
Structural Engineering Team Members: Bonghwan Kim, Dohwan Kong, Georgi Petrov
Team Members: Kat Park, Lauren Bass
Architect of Record: SAMOO Architects & Engineers
MEP Engineering: Syska Hennessy Group
Sustainable Design: Buro Happold
Fire and Life Safety: Schirmer Engineering
Lighting Design: Susan Brady Lighting Design SBLD
Landscape: Thomas Balsley Associates
Vertical Transportation: Van Deusen & Associates

**King Abdullah Financial District Conference Center**
**Riyadh, Saudi Arabia**
**Designed 2011**

Client: Rayadah Investment Company
Design Partner: Roger Duffy
Managing Partner: Peter Magill
Project Manager: Joseph Ruocco
Senior Designer: Scott Duncan
Senior Technical Architect: Eric Van Epps
Technical Coordinator: Daniel Fletcher
Senior Building Enclosure Architect: Reiner Bagnato
Specifications: Herbert Lynn
Senior Architectural Field Representative: Sunil Mistry
Senior Structural Field Representative: Tony Maalouf
Team Members: Evan Jenkins, Blake Altshuler, Chiara Pongiglione, Leigh Jester, Kat Park
Structural Consultant: Charles Besjak, Preetam Biswas, Georgi Petrov, Nathaniel Gonner, Aurelie Ble Tanmoy Chowdhury, Michael Berger, Ali Lame, Xiaoyu He
Design Assist/Superstructure & Curtain Wall Fabricator: Permasteelisa Gartner
Mechanical Consultant: WSP Flack + Kurtz
Landscape Consultant: HM White
Lighting/IT/Telecom/Audio-Visual Consultant: EXP
Water Features Consultant: Aqua Design International
Fire and Life Safety Consultant: Rolf Jensen & Associates, Inc.
Vertical Transportation Consultant: Van Deusen & Associates
Kitchen/Food Service Consultant: Hopkins Food Service
Signage/Wayfinding Consultants: C&G Partners, LLC
Acoustical Services: Shen Milsom & Wilke
Cost Estimating Consultant: Ward Williams Associates

**The Planning of Four Villages on University Island**
**Guangzhou, China**
**Designed 2008–09**

Client: Guangzhou University Town Management Committee
Design Partner: Philip Enquist
Design Director: Douglas Voigt
Managing Partner: Richard F. Tomlinson II
Project Manager: Aaron May
Team Members: Jae Min Lee, Jennifer Skowlund, John Law, Javier Gil Vieco, Lulu Zhang, Naifei Sun
Village Representatives: Beigang, Nanting, Suishi and Beiting village leaders
Local Design Institute: Panyu Architecture and Planning Institute

**Poly International Plaza**
**Beijing, China**
**Designed 2010–12**

Client: Beijing Poly Ying Real Estate Development Co. Ltd.
Managing Partner: Gene Schnair
Design Director: Leo Chow
Technical Director: Keith Boswell
Structural Design Director: Mark Sarkisian
Project Manager: Larry Chien
Senior Design Architect: Angela Wu
Design Architect: Brian Mulder
Technical Coordinator: Brian Cook
Project Coordinator: Stephanie Chang
Team Members: Christopher Talbott, Edward Rendel, Meehae Kwon, Lisa Hedstrom, Chaelyun Lee, Justin Ho, Rikako Wakabayashi, Peter Albertson, Tim Watters, Jeffrey Bajamundi
Senior Structural Engineer: Neville Mathias
Structural Engineering Team: Rupa Gurai, Andrew Krebs, Zhaofan Li, Joanna Zhang, Jeffrey Keileh, Christopher Horiuchi, Danny Bentley, Feliciano Racines

Senior Interior Designer: Tamara Dinsmore
Interior Design Team: Frederica Carrara
MEP Consultant: WSP Flack + Kurtz
Landscape Consultant: SWA Group
Lighting Consultant: Francis Krahe & Associates Inc.
Green Building Design Consultant: Built Ecology
Vertical Transportation: Edgett Williams Consulting Group

**United States Air Force Academy Center for**
**Character and Leadership Development**
**Colorado Springs, Colorado**
**Designed 2010–12**

Client: United States Air Force Academy
Design Partner: Roger Duffy
Managing Partner: Anthony Vacchione
Senior Designers: Scott Duncan, Frank Mahan
Project Manager: Mark Leininger
Technical Coordinator: Thierry Landis
Director, Structural Engineering: Charles Besjak
Associate Director, Sustainable Engineering Studio: Teresa Rainey
Structural Engineer: Preetam Biswas
Senior Mechanical Engineer: Joseph DiLenno
Team Members: Christian Kotzamanis, Peter Glasson, Jing Hao, Natalie Langone
Sustainability Specialist: Megan Inouye
Structural, Civil, MEP, Sustainability: Skidmore, Owings & Merrill LLP
Landscape Architect: THK Associates, Inc.
Code/Fire Safety: CCI
IT/ Acoustics / AV: Cerami & Associates
Cost Estimating: Faithful+Gould
Lighting Design: Brandston Partnership, Inc.
Theater Consultants: Fisher Dachs Associates
Historic Preservation: Robert Nauman
Topographic Survey: Nolte Associates, Inc.
Wind Tunnel Testing: RWDI

**Image Credits**
All images courtesy of SOM unless otherwise noted.
We have made every effort to find all copyright holders.
However, should we have omitted to contact copyright
holders in any individual instances, we would be most
grateful if these copyright holders would inform us
forthwith.


**Acknowledgments:**
The Partners of SOM extend their thanks to the
Editorial Board, Peter MacKeith, the Jurors, and to all
those who have contributed to the represented work.
We would also like to thank Scott Duncan, Blake
Altshuler, Carolina Burdo, Tong Tong, Nurdan Kilic,
Sergio Difilippi, Olin McKenzie, Brian Ha, and Lydia
Teunisen, in assembling, writing, and coordinating the
materials for this *SOM Journal 8*.

Edited by Peter MacKeith

Editorial board: Peter MacKeith, Joan Ockman,
Luis Fernández-Galiano

Managing editor: Amy Gill

Copyediting: Eugenia Bell, Tas Skorupa

Chinese translation: Tong Tong

Graphic design: SOM

Typesetting and reproductions:
Weyhing digital, Ostfildern

Typeface: Arial MT

Production: Nadine Schmidt, Hatje Cantz

Printing: sellier druck GmbH, Freising

Paper: Nopacoat matt, 150 g/m$^2$

Binding: Conzella Verlagsbuchbinderei,
Urban Meister GmbH, Aschheim-Dornach

Published by
Hatje Cantz Verlag
Zeppelinstrasse 32
73760 Ostfildern
Germany
Tel. +49 711 4405-200
Fax +49 711 4405-220
www.hatjecantz.com
Hatje Cantz books are available internationally at
selected bookstores. For more information about our
distribution partners, please visit our website at
www.hatjecantz.com.

ISBN 978-3-7757-3450-9

Printed in Germany